Your Invisible Enemy
Your Invisible Power

*How to recover from your
dysfunctional childhood and live
the life you want*

Loreen McKellar

Clink Street

London | New York

Published by Clink Street Publishing 2020

Copyright © 2020

First edition.

The author asserts the moral right under the Copyright, Designs and Patents Act 1988 to be identified as the author of this work.

All rights reserved. No part of this publication may be reproduced, stored in a retrieval system or transmitted, in any form or by any means without the prior consent of the author, nor be otherwise circulated in any form of binding or cover other than that with which it is published and without a similar condition being imposed on the subsequent purchaser.

ISBN: 978-1-913568-12-2 – paperback
978-1-913568-13-9 – ebook

Utis B and Taye B – Missing You
Don Mac – You were right. I apologise.
With love to all my babies
and
With deepest thanks and gratitude to
The Solicitor (non-practising)

+ to my friend
Jackie
So glad we have met.
love Lereen xx

Contents

Preface		v
Introduction		1
1.	The Law of Attraction	3
2.	The Fight-or-Flight Response	9
3.	Adverse Childhood Experiences (ACEs)	16
4.	Dangerous Families – the Hidden Epidemic	23
5.	Attachment, Regulation, and the Need for Nurture	29
6.	The Romanian Orphans	35
7.	Brain Structure Function Deficits Cause Dysfunctional Behaviour	41
8.	The Suppression of Negative Emotions	47
9.	Core Behaviours – Normal Reactions to Abnormal Situations	59
10.	How Your Brain Blocks Your Efforts to Use the Law of Attraction	75
11.	The Space Age of Abundance	78
12.	How the Invisible Enemy Holds You Back	80
13.	Time for Healing	86
Closing Thought		95
Appendix		96
References		99
Suggested Reading		105

Preface

As the train sped towards me, I wondered at exactly what point I should just fall forward. I wanted it to be a quick death and I didn't want the driver to have time to apply the brake.

Yes, I was depressed. I was at the bottom of a deep hole, and at that moment I felt death would be a welcome release from my grim existence.

But I did not kill myself. Something inside of me said, "Your life may be miserable, but you don't want to end it. Stay alive. There's a way forward." I stepped back from the line, physically and metaphorically. Somewhere deep down I had a bigger picture of my life, one that suggested life was too precious to lose.

I watched as the train rolled into the station. The doors opened and people got on and off as they always did. No one noticed or cared about my problems. They had things to do and places to go. Resigned to living, I put one foot in front of the other and got on with my day.

Thankfully, I'm still alive, and I've put those times behind me. During my long journey of survival and healing, I've often thought, "Why? Why do I feel this way, when so many other people go about their business without a care in the world? Why am I different?" I'm sure you've had the same feelings. You've probably said to yourself, "It would be great to feel happy and positive! So what's my problem? Why can't I just *be* happy like everyone else?"

It wasn't a sudden whim that led me to the train station, ready to jump. In my life—as it well may be in yours—my descent into despair didn't happen overnight. Over time, I was able to figure out that it was a combination of adverse childhood experiences (ACEs) from my past and present-day stressors that led me to that dark place.

I'll talk more about adverse childhood experiences in the pages ahead. For the stressors, let me take you back to 2008. The worldwide financial crash meant my income was cut in half. To service my large home mortgage, I had been working fourteen-hour days, and suddenly even that wasn't enough. I also had to service the mortgage on my rental property, which had been turned into a drug den, and the ringleader (my tenant) was in prison. His mates decided to use the property as a free-for-all.

In the middle of this, suddenly my employer informed me I was not doing my job to the company's satisfaction. After fifteen years of consistently well-reviewed service, they put me on "performance management review," which meant my work would be scrutinised every day.

The pressure began to overwhelm me.

What really lay behind the alleged concern of the management team was that they wanted to reduce headcount. Across the board, employees were being faced with being "managed out." This was a euphemism for bullying and belittling a person, hoping to get an individual to flounce out of their job before he or she would need to be paid to leave.

Every day before work, I prayed that I would be able to leave the company in a sober and peaceful manner. Flouncing out had been my trump card in the past. I would get petulant at a slight, whether real or perceived, and hand in my notice. But this time, I envisaged myself walking out of the firm with my head held high. I would stroll off into the sunshine, ready to commence a new chapter in my life.

To do this effectively, I needed to get tough with the company. I sought legal advice, which led to them back-pedalling. Subsequently, I passed the review. I only lasted another eight months, but at least they gave me an acceptable payoff.

Unfortunately, I was in debt for nearly £350,000. The mortgage companies were threatening repossession and calling in bailiffs.

I had crashed.

I prayed and I meditated. I asked for the courage and resilience to do what I was responsible for.

I realised I had not been treating the rental of the house as a business. I hadn't been taking it seriously.

This was a typical behaviour blip of mine. I would start something and then back away if it got too difficult. I saw life in shades of black and white. If it was easy, I'd do it. If it was hard, I'd abandon the project and run away. I was addicted to what was exciting and new. This led me to never achieving very much beyond a certain point.

By using the methods I reveal in this book, strengthening my resilience, and using prayer and meditation, I eventually got the courage to evict the tenants and change all the locks. I held their big television screen and their variety of designer trainers for ransom until they paid me some back rent. Yes, I had to get nasty. I realised fairy dust wasn't going to work. In terms of the law of attraction, I had to act in a negative manner: fight fire with fire.

I cleaned up the property and moved in a family who have lived there, happily, for over eight years. And, my rent is paid on time. Positive result!

This story isn't all about money; far from it. Cash flow was not my only challenge, and your own difficulties and suffering may have nothing to do with financial worries. But in all problems that threaten to overwhelm, the focal point is where the deep emotional roots have developed and have grown into something unmanageable. By committing to addressing the roots, however uncomfortable it gets, you can begin to move on to where, and how, change takes place.

In this period of soul searching, I came to a startling realization: My brain had been *resisting happiness*.

It sounds absurd, doesn't it? After all, what kind of person would prefer pessimism over hope? Misery over gladness? Wouldn't any rational person want to attract positive energy and material comfort?

Perhaps. But somehow, and for some reason, I hadn't been taking the rational approach to life. Once I understood why my brain was so resistant to accepting happiness, the law of attraction began to work for me. I made myself change my thinking. Lo and behold, as the difficulty with the tenants eased, simultaneously I got extra hours of work, won cash on local lotteries, received money after a relative died, and for my spare room got a lodger who paid on time, every time. I received loan insurance repayments from my banks. I was gifted money by friends whom I then helped with getting insurance repayments. I helped with issues from parking tickets to dealing with banks after a death, and received a lunch, gift certificate, or cash in an envelope as recompense. In short, I became known as someone who could write letters that got results.

I only discovered these gifts, up to then lying latent within me, when I took responsibility for my interactions with the world.

Then I got a health scare. As I began to recover on a

financial level from my problems with the tenants and my spiralling debts, I developed an autoimmune disease, in which the body, for various reasons, attacks itself.

The consultant felt the only solution was to remove a gland in my throat. I asked him to give me six weeks. He agreed. During that time, I drank green drinks, had colon cleanses, exercised, and ran a 10K race. I prayed. I visualised myself healthy and well. Whilst I had once abandoned myself, now I was strong enough to take responsibility for my mental and physical health.

I admitted to myself that I was scared and powerless. I reached out for support from allies, whom I will detail in this book. From them I received positive, practical, and productive energy that I didn't know had been around me all the time.

When I returned to see the consultant, he said my counts were in the healthy range. The operation was no longer necessary. I should stop taking my medication.

At this point, I give you a quote from American author and motivational speaker Jim Rohn, which I love: "Don't ask for the situation to get easier; ask that you become stronger."

In other words, each time you meet an obstacle, if you want to overcome it, you must change. This is at odds with some teachings where you demand the world changes and delivers what *you* want. You need to be able to change to meet the challenge in front of you.

When I lived through a lens of fear, lacking the ability to act, I attracted bailiffs, debt, and bad health. The new confident, proactive person attracted positive events and experiences that mirrored my new self-image. This new image has stuck, as it is grounded in healing from the inside and positive feedback from the world.

To understand why my mind had stubbornly refused to

embrace peace and contentment, I started learning about the brain and how it grows and develops. I learned that the brain is a very delicate instrument, and as it matures it's subject to a wide variety of forces, both internal and external. When you're growing up, all the good things that happen to you help shape your brain, and all the bad things that happen have an equal effect.

The part that can be hard to understand is that these changes to the development of your brain, and even your brain in adulthood, can be long-lasting. They can stay with you for years and even decades. How you feel about yourself and the world around you can be influenced, or even dictated, by any physical or emotional trauma you experienced years earlier.

As I learned more, I concluded it would be useful to share my experiences and insights with others who find themselves in the same dark place. With this book, my aim is to help you connect to a time in your past you may not even remember, and to reconnect with it, and begin the process of healing. I want to facilitate the "dropping of the penny," to help you to see not only *what* is happening in your adult life, but *why* it is happening.

On that day at the train station, I stepped back from the line. I've written this book because I want to help you to step back from the line too.

Introduction

Are you one of the many followers of the law of attraction who are not achieving their dreams and goals? Despite your best efforts, do you find your negative thinking hijacks your thoughts? Do you sometimes feel there's an invisible enemy inside you blocking your path to the things in life you desire and envision?

If you answer "yes," then I want you to know you're not alone. The law of attraction has been taught since the late nineteenth century, yet over a century later even John Assaraf, presenter in the film, *The Secret*, put the manifestation failure rate at 99 per cent.

The time has come for a new approach. Life is moving fast: technology which ten years ago was the stuff of science fiction is now in our homes and our pockets. All this advancement came from the minds of humans. People just like you are envisioning new ideas and making them a reality.

You can see the possibilities for a better life, but there's a problem. You feel you're not tapping into the positive energy that's lifting everyone else. As you struggle to use the law of attraction for your own benefit, you wonder, "Why are so many people using their minds to send our fellow humans into space and achieve other wondrous things, while I'm stuck in first gear, unable to get out of the garage?"

Hitherto, the information about achieving abundance and prosperity was ethereal and otherworldly. The dismal results make it clear that just putting up your vision board is not enough.

In this book, I'm going to reveal the powerful forces that may be holding you back. Often they take the form of ACEs or traumas. These can have a lasting, physical effect on your brain. That's right: prolonged or acute stress can change the structure of your brain and make it more difficult for you to visualise and focus on the images of success at the core of the law of attraction. You may *think* you want success (however you define it), but because of the damage done by trauma and stress, you *don't feel you deserve* success. To get what you want requires sustained effort, but you can't keep the positive image in your mind long enough to reach it. The invisible enemy—which is secretive but powerful—tries to knock you off course. It tells you that failure is a more comfortable way to live than success, and that unhappiness is all you're entitled to.

This book will show you, step by step, how you can identify your invisible enemy, confront it, and take away its power. With your newfound freedom, you can make the law of attraction work for you and set your sights on a life of sunlight and happiness.

Ready? Let's get started!

Chapter 1
The Law of Attraction

The mind is a powerful thing.

All that we have created in our world—from the commonplace paper clip to the mighty skyscraper, from a child's doodle to a great work of art, from the ancient abacus to the most powerful supercomputer—began as an idea in the human imagination. The intent of the idea was to *make life better*.

Eons ago, a caveman thought, "I'll bet fire would make our lives easier. Let's give it a try!"

Thousands of years later, someone thought, "What if I put a sail on my boat? Then I could travel much further and faster!"

In our own time, someone proposed, "Let's build a portable computer that anyone can use at home or in their office!"

All of these ideas were the result of *positive thinking*. They had their genesis in the belief that life is worth living, and it can get better, and by dreaming and taking action we can make it better.

Imagine for a moment a world in which we humans were incapable of envisioning a world where we lived longer, acquired more wealth, or simply had more fun than we did yesterday. What a dreary place that would be! We'd probably still be content to live in caves and wear smelly animal hides.

In fact, one thing that separates us from the other animals is that humans are the only species capable of imaging a better future and taking action to make it a reality. For all their intelligence, apes and dolphins and other smart animals cannot do this. They live today the same way they lived a thousand years ago. They don't make any progress.

There are many names for this unique ability that we humans possess. Many people call it "positive thinking." Others call it "optimism," because you envision the world being a better place tomorrow than it is today.

In recent times, we've heard a lot about "the law of attraction" and its ability to give you a life of wonderful design.

The concept has its roots in the early nineteenth century and the teachings of Phineas Quimby. Early in his life, Quimby was diagnosed with tuberculosis. At that time there was no cure for the disease, and well-meaning physicians offered all sorts of treatments designed to alleviate the symptoms. Quimby started a program of vigorous horseback riding, and he noticed that because he was *acting* like a healthy person, he began to *feel* like a healthy person. This method for easing his pain and seemingly subsequent recovery prompted Phineas to pursue a study of "Mind over Body." Here is part of what he wrote on the subject: "The trouble is in the mind, for the body is only the house for the mind to dwell in, and we put a value on it according to its worth. Therefore if your mind has been deceived by some invisible enemy into a belief, you have put it into the form of a disease, with or without your knowledge. By my theory or truth, I come in contact with your enemy and restore you to your health and happiness. This I do partly mentally and partly by talking till I correct the wrong impressions and establish the Truth, and the Truth is the cure."

By "some invisible enemy," Phineas may very well have been referring to an adverse childhood experience, about which I'll talk much more in the pages ahead. If you're an adult, it's entirely possible that this trauma has been shoved into an obscure corner of your memory, and you have no conscious awareness of its link to your present unhappiness.

The first person to use the term "law of attraction" was the Russian occultist Helena Blavatsky, who in 1877 wrote in her book *Isis Unveiled* that "attraction" was a powerful cosmic force. She said, "By whatsoever name the physicists may call the energizing principle in matter is of no account; it is a subtle something apart from the matter itself, and, as it escapes their detection, it must be something besides matter. If the law of attraction is admitted as governing the one, why should it be excluded from influencing the other?"

The idea became more widely known with the New Thought movement of the late nineteenth century. New Thought holds that Infinite Intelligence, or God, is everywhere, true human selfhood is divine, sickness originates in the mind, and "right thinking" has a healing effect. Many writers and philosophers explored the concept's thoughts and beliefs being linked to the physical world. One influential writer was James Allen, author of *As a Man Thinketh*, published in 1903. The opening lines of the book are:

> Mind is the Master power that moulds and makes,
> And Man is Mind, and evermore he takes
> The tool of Thought, and, shaping what he wills,
> Brings forth a thousand joys, a thousand ills: —
> He thinks in secret, and it comes to pass:
> Environment is but his looking-glass.

The twentieth century produced many bestselling books based on the law of attraction, including *Think and Grow Rich* (1937) by Napoleon Hill, *The Power of Positive*

Thinking (1952) by Norman Vincent Peale, and *You Can Heal Your Life* (1984) by Louise Hay.

It was in 2006 that the concept exploded internationally with the release of the film *The Secret*. This Australian documentary and the subsequent publication of the book by the same name catapulted the law of attraction into public discourse. In three months the book sold 1.75 million copies, plus 1.5 million DVDs. Executive producer Rhonda Byrne told *Newsweek* that her inspiration for creating *The Secret* came from reading the 1910 book *The Science of Getting Rich* by Wallace D. Wattles. *The Secret* didn't merely assert that having a positive viewpoint is good and healthy, and will bring you happiness; the book went further and claimed that you can manipulate *objective physical reality* through your thoughts and feelings. Other gurus advocate that just thinking of the things you want, and really focusing on them with all of your intention, is enough to harness the law of attraction and get what you want, always.

In other words, if you want a diamond ring, you need only picture it in your mind, and you will have it.

How's that working out for you? It's not, is it? Yet there can be no doubt that if you expect good things for yourself, you will seize them when they present themselves. Conversely, if you expect bad things for yourself, you will fail to seize upon the good opportunities that come your way.

I'll give you an example. In my preface I revealed that I owned a rental property, and that I had allowed it to be taken over by squatters who failed to pay their rent and who trashed the place. Therefore, for a period of time, this rental property was a negative force in my life.

But this was because I *expected* and *accepted* it as something negative!

To explain, let's turn back the clock to the first day I

put the property on the market. On that day, what if I had told myself this: "This rental property is going to make me a solid profit! It's going to improve my life. It's going to be an amazing investment, and nothing is going to make it otherwise."

Would I have then attracted a drug dealer? Would I have attracted rent arrears? Would I have attracted that kind of negativity into my life?

Of course not.

Later on, when I had realigned my thinking to seek and allow positivity, I transformed the rental property into the positive asset it should have been all along.

Think about it. We all know people who seem to throw away opportunities to improve their lives.

We all know the man who meets and dates a wonderful, attractive, upwardly mobile woman… and then he finds a way to pick a fight, so she leaves him, which he then complains about.

The woman who lands a good job that pays well… and then gets fired for not showing up. She then whines about how unfair life can be.

The person who wins the lottery… and then throws the money away and ends up broke. (Statistically, this happens more often than you may imagine!) You think, how could they do that? Why couldn't they use the windfall to make a better life for themselves?

Call it the law of attraction or the power of positive thinking, but there is no doubt that people who succeed are those who are able to visualise success, work for it, and, when it comes, embrace it.

The key phrase is, *"able to visualise success."* Remember the words of Quimby, who wrote, "If your mind has been deceived by some invisible enemy into a belief, you have put it into the form of a disease, with or without your knowledge." So many times, despite our best efforts, we fail to embrace what is good. We *say* we want success, we *think* we want a good life, and we *feel badly* when we fail, but yet we keep repeating the same behaviours.

Why?

As this book will reveal, inside you there could be an "invisible enemy" sabotaging your efforts to attract positive energy into your life. This invisible enemy is not something you consciously or willingly created. It became a part of you by virtue of forces that were beyond your control. But you have the power to identify it, recognise the damage it's doing and how it's holding you back, and take action to eliminate it, therefore opening yourself up to positive energy and a better future.

Chapter 2
The Fight-or-Flight Response

The law of attraction is based on a very simple idea: If you can imagine something and hold that image in your mind, then the likelihood of that thing entering your life is increased.

The law of attraction presupposes that what you *want* is something positive and good. It does not presume the image you form in your mind will be one in which you believe you deserve to be abused, or you deserve to be sick, or you deserve to be morbidly obese. After all, who would want that?

The law of attraction also presupposes that you are *capable* of forming in your mind an image that's positive and good. In cosmic terms, it assumes that you're able to connect with the positive energy of the universe and get in alignment with it, and let it guide you into a bright future.

But what if your brain doesn't want to cooperate? What if your hormones that govern how you feel about yourself are stuck in a "fight-or-flight" overdrive, preventing you from focusing on positive thoughts? What if you see the world as a dangerous place, full of traps and pitfalls, and it takes all of your energy to simply survive?

Anyone who has suffered from depression or anxiety knows the feeling of being told by "normal" people to "just snap out of it," or "pull yourself together." Or they say, "Why can't you just *be happy?*"

The answer may very well be, "My brain has been wired to be unhappy, and I cannot change it any more than I can change the colour of my eyes or how tall I am."

To explain how this can happen, we need to learn about brain structure and chemistry.

The brain has three areas:
1. The primitive brain, dealing with survival: fight/flight/freeze responses, food, and safety.
2. The limbic brain, dealing with emotions and attachment. The need for attachment is an innate part of a child's development. It is through attachment the child learns to modulate its feelings and to handle stress.
3. The triune brain, which handles executive functioning: language, thinking, logic, and creativity.

The three areas of the brain are interdependent. So positive thinking and negative thinking will use all three areas. For instance, to think positively we must feel safe, we must feel balanced in our emotions, and we must be creative.

A thought came to me during my research that would suggest an unlikely link between the law of attraction and adverse childhood experiences. The law of attraction states what you give consistent thought to you will attract. If people have been living consistently—from childhood—with toxic stress, in an inner state of hypervigilance with their feelings and perception of the world controlled by embedded traumatic thoughts of fear, disconnection and shame, what could they attract as their outer reality?

More of the same.

Toxic Stress

Toxic stress disrupts the body's self-regulation system. When endured while growing up in a dysfunctional environment, it overwhelms the body's coping mechanisms and damages the self-regulatory systems necessary to restore the body to its previous state. These systems involve a range of filtering systems in the central nervous system that help distinguish relevant from irrelevant stimuli. The areas of the brain connected with these systems are described below.

The Brainstem

The brainstem is called the primitive brain. For our work, we will call this area of the brain the subconscious brain. It controls our most base survival functions occurring beneath our level of conscious awareness, such as breathing and heart rate. It is also responsible for our emergency survival responses, which we call "fight, flight, or freeze."

The brainstem is found at the junction between the base of the brain and the spinal cord. Therefore the electrical and chemical impulses that carry messages from the brain through the central nervous system and from the system to the brain have a direct link, like a superhighway, down the spine and out into the organs in the body. This is the basis of the brain–body connection.

The brainstem has no emotional or logical ability. Its job is to control the mechanisms of aggression, repetitive behaviour, and our instinctive reactions such as fight, flight or freeze. Its focus is on survival and protecting you from danger without requiring conscious thought. Its responses are automatic.

The Limbic Brain

The limbic brain is a set of structures that deal with emotions and memory. They include:

Hypothalamus. This gland is concerned with homeostasis, which is returning something to a set point. It regulates anger and aggression, and hunger and thirst. It sends information and instructions to the body via the autonomic nervous system, and so has control of our subconscious behaviour such as blood pressure and breathing, especially in emotional circumstances. It also controls behaviour in the body via the pituitary gland, also called the "master gland," as it regulates important hormones involved in regulating growth and in our metabolism.

Hippocampus. The hippocampus is situated just above the brainstem. The close proximity means that interconnection and interaction between these areas is significant. The hippocampus moderates the amount of the steroid hormone cortisol in the bloodstream by signalling to the hypothalamus that the optimum level has been achieved. However, persistent high levels of cortisol damage the hippocampus, making it unable to feedback to the hypothalamus to tell it to stop creating cortisol. A compromised hippocampus will result in difficulty learning and remembering.

Amygdala. The amygdala is the control centre for defence responses such as "freezing behaviour, autonomic responses, suppression of pain, and stress hormone release" (LeDoux 1996.) Joe Dispenza identified four "highly charged primitive emotions" for which the amygdala is responsible: aggression, joy, sadness and fear. He also identified that the amygdala attached "different emotional charges to our long-term memories."

The amygdala stores memories along with its "perceptions" of the events that created the memories. The aim is to call on them to use as templates to assess the threat of future events and so help us avoid similar situations. Having this store of information and being part of our "fast and dirty" primitive emotional system (LeDoux 1996), the amygdala will subliminally process emotional stimuli and trigger a response below our conscious awareness. Without the correction and adjustment of a healthy frontal cortex, it will continue to drive fear or freeze responses. This can lead to a trauma sufferer experiencing flashbacks and symptoms of post-traumatic stress disorder (PTSD).

The Triune Brain

Prefrontal Cortex. This is the brain's moderator. It is in the third, and final, area of the brain to develop, the logical brain. It balances out the fight or flight response and the relaxation response based in our sympathetic and parasympathetic nervous systems. It is involved in developing executive functions such as mood and impulse control, working memory, decision-making, and self-regulation. If this area is fully developed, it also suppresses the response of the defensive amygdala, allowing you to be more adaptive in stressful or threatening situations. If the development of this area is disrupted, this disruption will cause anatomic changes and/or physiological dysregulations, which are "the roots of chronic, stress-related physical and mental illness" later in life (Shonkoff et al., 2012)

This relates to devotees of the law of attraction because Shonkoff's research has "pinpointed the left prefrontal cortex, an area just behind the left forehead, as the place where brain activity associated with meditation is especially intense." If there is damage to this area, the individual will experience a disruption to their meditation and creative visualisation skills. This research suggests the trauma has caused physical damage leaving us without the healthy brain needed to manifest and create.

Further, the prefrontal cortex area of the brain conducts the higher order goal-planning and executing functions as well as self-discipline and self-motivation. These are at the heart of creative visualisation and the law of attraction. To turn ideas into reality, you need to visualise your goal and then take steps towards its achievement. Even if these steps are just letting others know of your aspirations, you are releasing energy around your desire, which will draw you towards opportunities and situations that lead you closer to your goal.

Cortisol. In states of high sensitivity and anxiety, the brain excretes cortisol, which has a very important role in helping the body respond to stress.

However, research has shown that repeated experience of excessive and sustained cortisol secretion can create hypersensitivity to stressors. This is because cortisol looks for receptors to which to bind. Toxic stress causes excess cortisol to be released. The excess cortisol causes receptors to become overused and so shut down. Therefore, when future stress events create cortisol, there are no receptors to which to bind. The cortisol then washes around the brain looking for a home, while mentally you feel this stressful feeling will never stop. Studies have linked depression in adults with such hyperreactive stress responses.

Research has found a strong link between cortisol dysfunction and the effect of insecure attachment to a primary caregiver (Gunnar et al., 1996.) Without someone to help a child manage the stress, and armed with underdeveloped inner resources, the child develops emotional insecurity. This is because children need to be taught how to manage their emotions and they need to receive regular emotional support and comfort from a caregiver. Further research has found that cortisol dysfunction impairs the immune system, the ability to assimilate new information, and the ability to relax. This leads to adults who are found to have an internal working model that is destructive. It was also concluded that the model was set up from early in life (Gerhardt, 2015).

What this means for us who want to achieve using the law of attraction is that when your brain tries to do the right thing and visualise something good, and tries to orient itself towards achieving it, our compromised brain, harbouring its "invisible enemy," can block the process and create confusion, leading to self-doubt and depression. It's a vicious cycle: you try to attract positive energy, but your brain blocks the feelings as they are unfamiliar and considers them a threat, which makes you depressed and increases the difficulty you will have to attract goodness into your life.

Chapter 3
Adverse Childhood Experiences (ACEs)

In the previous chapter we learned about how the brain works with the hormones in your body to accomplish certain tasks—specifically, how to get the brain and body "revved up" to respond to danger. This is the "fight-or-flight" response, and it's commonly described as a "cascade" of events that occur over time.

This self-defense cascade can occur in three stages. They are:

1. **Arousal**. When the threat first appears, the body prepares for action. Breathing and heart rate increase and muscles tense.

2. **Fight-or-flight**. As the threat continues, the body assumes an active defence response for dealing with threat. Fighting is one choice. (Your abusive husband comes home drunk, and you pick up the frying pan to defend yourself.) Flight is another choice. (Your abusive husband comes home drunk, and you lock the bathroom door.)

3. **Freezing**. This is an extreme inability to move or call out, and a shut down in the face of fear. For the victim, neither fight nor flight is seen as a viable choice. Both

are equally bad. It's like when the abusive spouse breaks down the bathroom door, and the victim's only choice is to be passive, freeze, and take the abuse; and also to shut down her emotions as a survival skill.

Another word for this is "disassociation," when you mentally remove yourself from the situation. Physiologically your blood retreats from the surface of your body into your core, keeping your vital organs working. Psychologically you shut down your emotions and you do not feel any pain. However, this can also translate into you being numb to your feelings long after the threat has passed.

These behaviours happen beneath our conscious awareness and are directed by the base brain and its aim to serve and protect.

Adverse Childhood Experiences

Children are more vulnerable to developmental problems and have little defence against physical and emotional abuse. For that reason, traumatic events that cause permanent physiological or psychological damage are called adverse childhood experiences (ACEs). In their effect on the individual they are similar to adult PTSD, which is most commonly seen in military personnel. Both terms refer to any number of long-lasting physiological changes to the brain as the result of prolonged stress or intense trauma.

However, PTSD is different in children specifically because the child's brain is still developing. A war veteran is two things: firstly, an adult with a fully developed brain, and secondly, trained for the experience of war. Research has shown that veterans who experienced childhood trauma are more susceptible to PTSD than their comrades who did not have such experiences (van der Kolk 2015).

The phrase "complex post-traumatic stress disorder" (CPTSD) has been coined to deal with the intricate links of experiences and emotions of childhood mental and emotional trauma. (Walker 2013.)

The importance of ACEs came to the forefront with the CDC-Kaiser Permanente Adverse Childhood Experiences Study, one of the largest investigations of childhood abuse, neglect, and household challenges on later-life health and well-being.

The original ACE Study was conducted from 1995 to 1997 by Kaiser Permanente, a major American integrated managed care consortium based in Oakland, California. In the study, over 17,000 volunteers completed a confidential Family Health History and Health Appraisal survey regarding their childhood experiences and current health status and behaviours.

After a series of questions about the respondent's current health and personal habits, the survey turned to the respondent's childhood experiences. For example, this set of questions asked about physical abuse. The reply choices ranged from "never" to "very often":

Sometimes parents or other adults hurt children. While you were growing up, that is, during your first 18 years of life, how often did a parent, step-parent, or adult living in your home:
- 58a Swear at you, insult you, or put you down?
- 58b Threaten to hit you or throw something at you, but didn't do it?
- 58c Actually push, grab, shove, slap you, or throw something at you?
- 58d Hit you so hard that you had marks or were injured?
- 58e Act in a way that made you afraid that you might be physically hurt?

Other questions dealt with sexual assault, alcoholism, drug use, smoking, suicide in the family, and other traumatic events or circumstances.

The researchers invented the ACE score to gauge a person's risk for chronic disease. Based on their survey answers, patients received one point for each type of trauma. The higher their score, the higher their risk of subsequent social and health problems.

The Centers for Disease Control and Prevention (CDC) analysed the data and concluded that ACEs correlated with health and psychological problems later in life. In other words, "as the number of ACEs increases so does the risk for negative [life] outcomes."

The result of growing up in an environment where there are sustained ACEs, such as loss of a parent or abuse, manifest in adult life as compulsive behaviours, depression, addictions, and an increased likelihood of cancers and autoimmune and liver diseases.

The ACE study showed that the bigger smash-ups and their resulting scars occurring in adulthood often have their roots in childhood.

Vincent Felitti's Discovery

In 1985, Vincent Felitti was chief of Kaiser Permanente's Department of Preventive Medicine in San Diego. He ran a weight-loss clinic, which every year enrolled roughly 1,500 overweight people. He had started the clinic in 1980 because many Kaiser Permanente members suffered from health problems, including heart attacks and diabetes, which were made worse by their excess weight. If they lost weight, they'd be healthier.

His problem was that more than half of the participants

dropped out before completing the program. He was particularly confused after reviewing their medical records, which revealed almost all of the dropouts had been *losing*, not gaining, weight. This was baffling. Why were people who were succeeding dropping out?

To shed light on the problem, Felitti asked many of those who had left the program if he could interview them, and 286 agreed. He soon learned two intriguing facts.

First, none of the participants had been born overweight. All had normal or below normal birth weights.

Second, participants who were severely obese tended to gain weight to a certain set point, and then their weight stabilised. If they lost weight, within weeks or months they typically regained all of it or more.

Felitti still didn't know why so many of his patients made the deliberate choice to be obese. It was as if this was what they wanted, despite the obvious risks to their health. In terms of the law of attraction, his patients were either incapable or unwilling to visualise themselves living life at a healthy weight. Their minds refused to grasp and hold what was plainly a positive goal.

In this case, the cause was as much psychological as it was hormonal.

One day, Felitti was interviewing yet another clinic dropout. He asked her a series of questions: How much did you weigh when you were born? In first grade? In high school? How old were you when you became sexually active? How much did you weigh when you married?

"I misspoke," he recalled to writer Jane Ellen Stevens in 2012. "Instead of asking, 'How *old* were you when you were first sexually active,' I asked, 'How much did you *weigh* when you were first sexually active?'"

The patient replied, "Forty pounds."

Not sure he had heard her correctly, he asked again.

Tearfully, she repeated her answer and added, "It was with my father."

Felitti was shocked—as far as he knew, incest was very rare. But when he started asking other patients, many more said the same thing: they had been sexually abused as children.

One of his interviewees said something that for Felitti was like a key opening a lock. This was a program dropout who had been raped when she was twenty-three years old. During the year after the attack, she gained over 100 pounds. "As she was thanking me for asking the question," Felitti told Stevens, "she looks down at the carpet, and mutters, 'Overweight is overlooked, and that's the way I need to be.'"

While conventional wisdom assumed that overeating—a major cause of obesity—was a *problem* that patients wanted to correct, in fact the behaviour was the *solution* to a bigger, underlying problem. The woman was consumed by CPTSD, and her brain had been altered so that she saw *any* sexual interaction as threatening, and the way to avoid the stress of such interactions was to try to make herself "unattractive" (at least in her own mind) and less of a target.

As a qualifying note, the study of ACEs does *not* assert that everyone who is overweight has been a victim of sexual abuse. Obesity is a complex disease, and there are many reasons why a person might be seriously overweight. But if you look at it from the other direction, there is no doubt that a traumatizing ACE—at any age—alters the brain and leads to behavioural changes that the individual takes to help themselves feel better.

The emergence of our knowledge of ACEs, CPTSD, and how the human mind responds to trauma or chronic stress has produced evidence that many self-destructive behaviours, including overeating, anorexia nervosa, bulimia, cutting, substance abuse, financial problems, sex addiction, and co-dependency, are strategies that give the individual short-term relief from a larger psychological problem. Subjects report a gratifying but temporary sense of relief when they engage in self-destructive behaviours, almost like pushing a "reset" button in their minds. To them, the short-term gain is well worth the long-term pain.

It's well to remember that one of the basic tenets of the law of attraction is that the positive things people visualise and strive for all tend to be of the same type—a mutually satisfying relationship, a productive career, a better house, a higher income. If your brain is programmed with negative images and feelings of a past trauma, then you will have difficulty holding other, positive images in your mind. It's not impossible; the world is full of people who have overcome difficult childhoods to become very successful. But for you and me, a high ACE score and the resulting damage to our brain health increases the likelihood of us being incapable of mustering up the focus and drive necessary to reach a positive goal.

Therefore the focus must be first and foremost on healing your brain and thus your inner world.

Chapter 4

Dangerous Families – the Hidden Epidemic

Sadly, for too many adults, the family was, and may still be, a dangerous place.

Growing up, no childhood is free from the occasional moment of pain or even terror. Every parent loses his or her temper once in a while. Every adult caregiver may, at one time or another, treat a child harshly. Nobody is perfect, and this is part of being human. However, with loving and supportive caregivers, those moments during which the fight-or-flight response is revved up can quickly pass, and normal homeostasis return.

Under such circumstances, the child can grow into adulthood with a mind free from invisible enemies. In the aggregate, the young person's memories will be pleasant and positive. The young person's self-image will include a vision of *future* success because there's a corresponding memory of *past* success. In the young person's mind there will be no dark voice whispering, "You do not deserve happiness and a positive life." Instead, when they asks themselves, "Can I do this task? Can I achieve this goal?" the answer will be a resounding "Yes!"

But if we're talking about abuse that can permanently affect a child and rise to the level of an ACE, we're basically talking about four things:

1. Sexual abuse. Sometimes it can take just one traumatic event to permanently affect a child's development. You can have a family that to an outsider appears perfectly normal and well adjusted, but if one incident of child rape, incest, or other abuse occurs, the child will be seriously damaged.

2. Physical abuse. In the old days, corporal punishment was considered routine, and even a good thing. ("Spare the rod and spoil the child.") Today we know differently. Research has shown that the only thing corporal punishment creates is a future adult who will do the same thing to his or her child, generation after generation, without end.

3. Toxic environment. Alcoholism, drug abuse, suicide, and witnessing domestic violence are all ACEs. When these are events that happen repeatedly, it gives the child no relief from her fight-or-flight response.

4. Neglect. Perhaps the most common form of child abuse, this is the ongoing failure to meet a child's basic needs. A child might be left hungry or dirty, or without supervision, shelter, proper clothing, or healthcare.

5. Emotional abuse. This is long-term, habitual abuse of the child and can be verbal. It can happen in any environment, including one of wealth and physical comfort. The parent tells the child he or she is worthless, or has no hope of succeeding, or isn't loved, or should never have been born. Or it can be based in emotional neglect where the child receives no support, is ignored or emotionally abandoned. When a person upon whom you depend for your very life and safety tells you these things, you take it as a real threat, and your fight-or-flight instinct responds accordingly.

Regardless of the family's level of income, children who are emotionally or physically neglected may grow up believing that no one cares about them. The effects may include poor brain development, excessive risk-taking, forming dangerous relationships, difficulty with relationships later in life, and a higher risk of mental health problems, including depression.

In every nation around the world live adults who have suffered ACEs. They have grown up with the invisible enemy inside them, blocking their efforts to visualise and manifest success in their lives. Researchers have even gone as far as to call child abuse a "hidden epidemic," as Bessel van der Kolk wrote in *The Body Keeps the Score: Brain, Mind, and Body in the Healing of Trauma*.

One of the most tragic and challenging aspects of family child abuse is that the vulnerable child often has no place to turn for help. When you're ten years old and you depend upon your parents for your food, clothing, and shelter—the fundamental requirements for life itself—and those same parents are abusing you, you have a powerful incentive to not make them more angry. You do not want them to reject you and (in your imagination, at least) turn you out of the house to fend for yourself in the bewildering world of adults, some of whom may be just as mean as your parents. So you cope in a variety of ways that I'll discuss in the pages ahead, by trying to please them, by telling yourself things really aren't so bad, by creating an alternative reality for yourself.

Meanwhile, your brain is rewiring itself to get in sync with the negativity of your reality. Its programme is that negativity is normal. Adjusting to this is the only way the child survives.

The Sad Story of Kurt Cobain

Sometimes even people who seem to be able to attract success are in fact keeping a dark secret.

When rock star Kurt Cobain committed suicide at the age of twenty-seven, he left behind a highly profitable music career in the form of his band Nirvana, as well as a wife and young child. Rising to the top of any industry is difficult, but in just a few short years Cobain had transformed himself from the frontman of an obscure garage band to an international superstar.

A reading of his life story, however, reveals that if Cobain had taken the ACE test, he would have scored very high. Members of his family had a sad history of suicide, mental illness, and alcoholism. Two of Kurt's uncles had committed suicide, both with guns. Studies show that even one suicide in a family is a significant ACE for the survivors, and puts other members of that family at higher risk for suicide.

After Kurt shot himself, his cousin Beverly Cobain, herself a mental health professional, said of her childhood, "Alcoholism runs rampant in the Cobain family. When I was growing up there was always alcohol and violence in our home." At a young age, Kurt was diagnosed with attention deficit disorder (ADD), then later with bipolar disorder. "His risk was very high," she said. "Untreated bipolar disorder, drug addiction, prior suicides of family members, alcohol, violence and unpredictability in his childhood, poor self-esteem, violence in his married life. Kurt could have been a poster child for risk of suicide."

The words of Kurt and his own family paint a grim picture of his childhood.

"Everything that Kurt did was a reflection on Don," said his mother, Wendy, about his father, whom she divorced when Kurt was nine years old. "If Kurt played badly at a baseball game, his father would just be infuriated after that game to the point where he'd just humiliate Kurt... He would knuckle-rap Kurt and call him a dummy. He'd just get irritated really quickly and—whack! over the head. My mom says she remembers a time when he actually threw Kurt clear across the room when he was like six."

Despite the abuse, Cobain claimed that he was basically a happy kid until his parents divorced, telling British rock journalist Jon Savage, "I had a really good childhood, until the divorce. Then, all of a sudden, my whole world changed. I became antisocial."

This assertion is interesting, because by any rational standard a child who suffers the abuse that Kurt Cobain did is unlikely to feel they had a "really good childhood"—unless as a survival mechanism the child has suppressed the feelings of fear and rage that have grown within him. When you're abused like that, and you have no way out (Cobain's mother was no help—she was an enabler of the abuser), then pretending to be happy is your ticket to survival. You live in a state of denial. But meanwhile, the invisible enemy is flexing his muscles and growing stronger within you.

Later in the book, we'll talk about how you can safely come out that kind of denial.

At school, Cobain said, "I was a scapegoat, but not in the sense that people picked on me all the time. They didn't pick on me or beat me up because I was already so withdrawn by that time. I was so antisocial that I was almost insane. I felt so different and so crazy that people just left me alone."

By the time he became an adult, Kurt Cobain's mind was so full of alienation and despair that the law of attraction simply wouldn't work for him. His material success—which is so often the focus of what we envision for ourselves—didn't make him happy. Sadly, like so many other people who take their own lives, whether intentionally or by extreme self-abuse, the ultimate act of self-abandonment was the only way he felt he could find peace.

Chapter 5
Attachment, Regulation, and the Need for Nurture

"The three environmental conditions absolutely essential to optimal human brain development are nutrition, physical security, and consistent emotional nurturing," wrote Gabor Maté in *The Realm of Hungry Ghosts* (2008). "The third prime necessity—emotional nurture—is the one most likely to be disrupted in Western societies. The importance of this point cannot be overstated: emotional nurturance is an absolute requirement for healthy neurobiological brain development."

John Bowlby's theory of attachment sees a baby's need for its primary caregiver as "a deep and enduring emotional bond that connects one person to another across time and space" (Ainsworth, 1973.) To be fed and housed is not enough for a child to develop into a healthy adult. If a child is held and actively nurtured by a responsive adult regularly, this will cause optimal social and mental health outcomes.

A child is born with a need to form an emotional attachment to a primary caregiver. The caregiver's role is to interact with the child in a positive manner. This interaction energetically regulates the child's internal arousal states. By attuning to the child using visual, facial, and auditory communication and gestures, the caregiver and child will learn to appropriately respond to the rises and falls in the emotions the child experiences. The caregiver also helps re-establish swiftly any lost rhythm, which allows the child to recover from stress and feel safe.

Having good enough care "supports an expansion of the child's coping capacities… and is a primary defence against trauma-induced psychopathology." (van der Kolk, 2015.)

Attachment Patterns

Secure attachment. "Such children feel confident that the attachment figure will be available to meet their needs. They use the attachment figure as a safe base to explore the environment and seek the attachment figure in times of distress" (Main & Cassidy, 1988).

Insecure avoidant. These children "are very independent of the attachment figure both physically and emotionally" (Behrens, Hesse, & Main, 2007). "They do not seek contact with the attachment figure when distressed. Such children are likely to have a caregiver who is insensitive and rejecting of their needs" (Ainsworth, 1979).

Insecure ambivalent. These children have received an inconsistent level of response to their needs from the primary caregiver. The child develops no feelings of security from the attachment figure. When distressed, they are difficult to soothe and are not comforted by interaction with the attachment figure.

Gabor Maté saw attachment patterns as multigenerational and passed down from parent to child. The attachment pattern he states can be seen in a child as young as one year old.

Experience-Expectant and Experience-Dependent

The list of behavioural symptoms arising from receiving less than good enough care during childhood is not exhaustive. All of them are based on the child not getting certain needs met. These needs are evolutionary. There are certain animals that can stand and look after themselves hours after birth. A human child, however, has been created with the need to experience care from its environment for years.

A child is born with the primitive brain that commands survival and deals with breathing, heartrate, and fight-or-flight behaviours. The structure of the limbic and triune brain develops after birth, and is both experience-dependent and experience-expectant. That is, the brain develops according to the experiences it both receives and does *not* receive in life (Berk et al., 2006).

If the child does not receive the necessary uplifting experiences, the primitive brain will be dominant, as the child's priority will be to meet his basic need to feel safe, to avoid feeling threatened, to move away from fear. If the child spends an extended time dealing with these basic needs, the child and the adult he or she becomes will lack development of the emotional and executive functioning areas of the brain.

Experience-expectant. For learning to take place, experience-expectant anticipates situations to occur. Neural networks in the brain expect specific stimuli to allow them to form. For instance, vision will develop as the eye is exposed to light and objects. If there is no exposure, vision will not develop. "Disruption of expectant sensory experience at the time the neurons are organizing and growing to meet that experience can cause irreversible damage" (Kagan & Herschkowitz, 2005).

Experience-dependent. A child's development is experience-dependent. Experience-dependent learning occurs in the home, school, and other environments. This learning requires that the brain be exposed to certain types of experiences consistent with its environment. The child can then develop the skills to survive in that environment. For instance, take language. For the first few months, a baby in an English-speaking home can distinguish between the sounds of a foreign language. She loses this ability by the end of her first year, and the language she hears at home has wired her brain for English.

In the same way, a child learns to regulate his emotions based on the feedback from his caregiver and his environment. His emotional experiences become embedded into the biological and inaccessible neurological systems. These are the nervous system and brain structure—the systems that underlie feelings and ways of perceiving and engaging with the world (van der Kolk, 20015). If the child's emotions become enmeshed with fear, disconnection, and shame because he experiences ongoing trauma, his emotions will be dominated by these feelings, and so distort both his inner and outer reality.

Growing up, we need those experiences to build specific circuits in our brain to help us develop the skills to manage the variety of feelings in life. We need these circuits if we are to motivate ourselves to follow through on our goals, negotiate with people practicing give and take, develop and maintain good relationships, communicate clearly, inspire and influence others, work well in a team, and manage conflict. We also must build the circuits to give us the ability to learn the skills to visualise creatively, meditate properly, and access our subconscious mind to benefit at will from the law of attraction.

Emotional Regulation and Emotional Trauma

"Emotional development continues throughout childhood and possibly throughout our lives. Emotional intelligence includes the ability to recognise one's emotions, handle those emotions, recognise others' emotions, and handle relationships. These characteristics can begin to be modelled from infancy" (Goleman et al., 2002).

A child learns about different feelings by experiencing a range of emotions. Rage, fear, and separation distress systems form at birth, readying the child for survival. In contrast, the traumatised child is not supported in building up his emotional repertoire (Sunderland, 2006). Attachment to a responsive caregiver is essential to help the child learn to control these systems and provide the child opportunities to learn how to calm herself. The prefrontal lobe helps control these emotions, but it develops after the emotional system. Therefore, the caregiving adult's frontal lobe helps the child learn to modulate its emotions and helps build the child's own frontal lobe.

Emotion and cognition are interlinked. Well-regulated emotions support executive functions such as:

- Emotional intelligence
    - Self-awareness
    - Self-regulation
    - Motivation
    - Social skills
    - Empathy

- Executive functioning
    - Cognitive flexibility – thinking about a situation in more than one way
    - Inhibitory control – ignoring distractions and resisting temptation

- Reflection – pause and think about challenges before taking action

Poorly controlled emotions interfere with the ability to learn and demonstrate these skills.

Harvard University (2006) found that "the foundations of social competence that are developed in the first five years are linked to emotional well-being and affect a child's later ability to functionally adapt in school and to form successful relationships throughout life."

A child must be taught how to manage his or her emotions. When there is a lack of support from a sensitive and responsible caregiver, the child will grow into an adult who does not know how to regulate his emotions. The anguish and confusion this lack of self-awareness causes results in him trying to regulate his feelings by behaviours or using substances.

Chapter 6
The Romanian Orphans

In the 1960s, the Communist Party in Romania decided that the country's population needed to be increased. In October 1966, Nicolae Ceaușescu made abortion illegal, contraceptives disappeared from store shelves, and secret police monitored all hospital procedures.

Within a year the number of births almost doubled and the estimated number of children per woman increased. The problem was that Romania was a poor country and most families had no way to support the sudden surge of babies. So the beleaguered parents put the children up for adoption, or abandoned them.

Over the next few decades, an estimated 170,000 children were raised in Romanian orphanages. Children were warehoused and given minimal food, clothing, and heat. The child–carer ratio was large, which meant the children received scant emotional nurturing.

The system of national orphanages persisted well into the new century. In the year 2000, a group of American researchers began a study of the Romanian orphanages and the children who lived in them.

When researcher Nathan Fox first entered the nursery of one of the state-run orphanages, as he later told the American Psychological Association, "The most remarkable thing about the infant room was how quiet it was, probably because the infants had learned that their cries were not responded to." Except when being fed, diapered, or bathed on a set schedule, the babies were confined to their cribs all day. For hours on end, they had little human contact. They weren't held or spoken to. Fox said that many simply stared at their own hands.

For the study, the researchers randomly assigned half of their subjects to move into Romanian foster families that had been determined to be healthy environments. The other half remained where they were, in the orphanage system.

Their investigation, the Bucharest Early Intervention Project, lasted fourteen years. They published their results in a book, *Romania's Abandoned Children: Deprivation, Brain Development, and the Struggle for Recovery*.

Over the course of the study, the researchers found differences in the behaviour and brain development between the two groups. The lack of care in the orphanage—essentially a massive ACE—created permanent brain damage to the Romanian children. On a brain scan of a Romanian orphan who was taken into institutional care not long after birth, the effects of deprivation at such a young age could be clearly identified. The neglect of the child had caused atrophy of the unused areas of the brain. If part of your body is not being constantly used, the brain will assume it is unnecessary to function and compensate somewhere else. If part of the brain has not been stimulated sufficiently, it goes "offline" or does not develop optimally.

Scans showed a lack of development of the emotional and executive functioning areas of the brains in the Romanian orphans because they did not receive proper or sustained emotional care. Scans of their brains showed there were gaps—literally holes—in the physical matter of the brain in the temporal lobe region, which is the area connected with emotions and sensory stimulation. The area had not developed because it had not been used. There was also a reduction in brain activity when compared to the activity of the brain of a child who received adequate care. It's thought that this damage leads to emotional and cognitive problems in adulthood.

Research was also undertaken on Romanian orphans who had been adopted. While they were better off than their peers left behind, they had significant problems too. Developmental assessments completed shortly after adoption were revealing, including "severe gross and fine motor, language and social delays." The children manifested substantial post-institutionalised behaviour, such as being unable to cry or express pain; or they showed sensory peculiarities, such as a preference to be wrapped tightly for sleeping.

After one year in their adoptive homes, many children showed a substantial catch-up in motor and language skills, which was happy news. But there remained developmental delays in language and fine and gross motor skills. There was still the absence of crying or expression of pain, which illustrated a disconnection from feelings. They also displayed difficulty attending to tasks and sleeping soundly, and sensory difficulties with loud noises, smells, and crowds, showing hypersensitivity. The children were not motivated—highlighting procrastination—and had difficulty concentrating on tasks, illustrating a lack of focus.

Does this behaviour sound familiar? Do you exhibit any such behaviours?

The major finding in the study was that a lack of nurturing in the Romanian orphans was associated with dysfunction in a group of limbic brain regions that deal with regulating the emotions. This area is activated by moderate stress, and significantly, it is damaged by prolonged stress.

This evidence is of critical importance. The neglect suffered by these children resulted in *physical damage* to the brain. The damage is not dissimilar to the brains of people who display autistic, attention deficit hyperactivity disorder (ADHD) or other attention deficit symptoms and of people who display compulsive or addictive behaviours—from the socially acceptable yet potentially life-threatening workaholism to the socially unacceptable yet potentially life-threatening substance abuse.

The message is clear: To grow properly and fully from infancy, the human brain needs emotional and environmental positive stimulation. Areas of the brain that do not receive enough stimulation literally do not grow properly. The brain is no different from a muscle: the more you use it, the stronger it gets.

Izidor Ruckel's Story

Izidor Ruckel was a Romanian boy who at the age of six months was placed in a state-run orphanage. He had polio that deformed his legs, and so his parents gave him to the Home Hospital for Irrecoverable Children (that's the actual name), where he joined 500 other castoffs.

In 1990, after the fall of the Berlin Wall and the opening of the Eastern Bloc, a crew from the ABC News show *20/20* arrived at the Home Hospital for Irrecoverable Children. After talking their way past the bewildered gatekeeper, they went inside with cameras rolling. It was not the first Romanian orphanage the news team had visited, but they quickly saw it was the worst.

"It was like an insane asylum," said Janice Tomlin, a producer who went inside. "We saw kids in straitjackets, we saw kids in a cage.... We saw this boy who was literally starving, dying."

Many of the orphans had shockingly low levels of brain activity. "Instead of a 100-watt light bulb, it was a 40-watt light bulb," said Charles Nelson.

Despite his crippled legs and stunted growth—he was ten years old but looked six—Izidor saw the American visitors as a ticket to freedom. One of the filmmakers, John Upton, said, "I remember Izidor literally grabbing my leg and making me sit down next to him. He told me through my interpreter that he wanted out of that hell."

The broadcast of the show created a huge groundswell of Americans seeking to adopt the abandoned kids. "My phone was ringing literally nonstop," said Tomlin, who later adopted two infant girls herself. "American couples called, all of whom had the saddest stories of trying to adopt, specifically wanting to adopt a particular child they had seen in our report."

The following year, at age eleven, an American family, Danny and Marlys Ruckel, adopted Izidor. He became an all-American boy, learning the language and adopting the culture. He also became a Christian.

But as he entered adolescence, darker impulses surfaced. "I got really homesick, I got really angry, I was not used to love," he recalled. "I became a hell child. I couldn't stand the family. I used to tell them, 'I want to go back to the orphanage.'"

He became belligerent, hitting his father and swearing at his mother. In his senior year he dropped out of high school and moved out of their house. He began smoking pot and drinking—classic tools of self-medication to ease the emotional pain—but he managed to keep his jobs at fast-food restaurants.

Of that time, Ruckel said, "I respond better when you beat me, or when you smack me around... That never happened. When you show me kindness, when you show me love, compassion, it seemed to make me even more angrier."

When he was eighteen, his family was involved in a serious car accident, and miraculously the event made him stop thinking of himself and his own problems. He reconciled with the Ruckels, quit doing drugs, and began attending church.

Izidor says he suspects the wiring in his brain was changed by his time in the orphanage. He now advocates for other orphans in Romania, and has formed Izidor Miniseries as well as written a book and produced two films. The strap line for his latest film, *Izidor*, is, "A disabled orphan escapes a hellish Romanian orphanage through adoption, only to grow up and discover he still isn't free." The brain and the body remember and keep you limited… and imprisoned.

Chapter 7
Brain Structure Function Deficits Cause Dysfunctional Behaviour

We will now look at the physical damage caused to the brain owing to sustained trauma in childhood, which is the cause of lack of success with the law of attraction.

Brain on Fire

The brain structure consists of three parts.

In a foetus, the brainstem, the first part of the brain, the primitive brain, is first detected at sixteen days gestation. Then the nervous system develops, then the organs.

The brainstem deals with our basic needs for survival. It takes in, sends out, and coordinates the brain's messages. Without conscious input, it controls many of the body's automatic functions, including breathing, heart rate, swallowing, digestion, and blood pressure. It has a direct link with all areas of the body through the intricate network that makes up the nervous system. If you receive appropriate nurturing as a child, parts two and three are the emotional brain and the logical brain will develop optimally. Together, their job is to moderate the base information coming from the brainstem. However, in a child receiving poor care and minimal emotional attachment, the brainstem remains in charge. It is inflamed and overworked. There is little or no tempering by the underdeveloped emotional and logical brains. The fearful information comes from the subconscious into the conscious mind unchecked and causes the child to act compulsively. In his book *The Emotional Brain* (1996) Le Doux sees this "quick and dirty" way of thinking as dangerous because it is not tempered by the logical brain.

In his book *Linchpin: Are You Indispensable?*, Seth Godin put it this way: "The lizard brain is hungry, scared, angry, and horny. The lizard brain only wants to eat and be safe. The lizard brain will fight (to the death) if it has to, but would rather run away. It likes a vendetta and has no trouble getting angry. The lizard brain cares what everyone else thinks, because status in the tribe is essential to its survival… The lizard brain is not merely a concept. It's real, and it's living on the top of your spine, fighting for your survival. But, of course, *survival* and *success* are not the same thing. The lizard brain is the reason you're afraid, the reason you don't do all you can. The lizard brain is the source of the resistance."

Left and Right Brain: Connection Lost

The three-part brain structure is then split into the left hemisphere and the right hemisphere.

The left hemisphere controls the right side of the body, and is the more academic and logical side of the brain.

The right hemisphere controls the left side of the body, and is the more artistic and creative side of the brain. It's responsible for intuition, creativity, deep feelings, and the ability to visualise and create images. In Schore (2009) he referenced Joseph (1992) who asserted the right brain and the emotional limbic system house the "childlike central core," which maintains all the memories and emotions that form one's self-image. Emotional responses in the brain are right brain dominant. The right hemisphere is responsible for generating self-recognition and self-love.

The primary pathway connecting the two hemispheres is a thick band of fibre called the corpus callosum. However, here there's more food for thought: Research has found that childhood abuse causes underdevelopment in the corpus callosum, which leads to deficient left-right brain integration.

"Our discoveries that abused patients have diminished right-left hemisphere integration and a smaller corpus callosum suggesting… they may shift between logical and rational state to highly emotional state. Lack of integration between the hemispheres may also be a factor in the genesis of dissociation" (Teicher 2000).

This lack of integration is definitely the main factor in the inability to manifest and use creative visualization. Many gurus stress linking the left and right brains. This will mean the logical and creative sides will work together to create solutions as we work towards our goals. If the two sides are not communicating with each other, this explains our "black and white" thinking and other core behaviours. This explains our inability to visualise and think creatively. The behaviours stem from a disordered brain structure.

A Very Grey Matter

What we call "grey matter" in the brain are the nerve cells called neurons. They are the most significant cells in the brain as they are the only cells that send messages via electrochemical signals to and from each other, and from the brain to and from the body. Research has shown that the more grey matter you have in the thought processing prefrontal cortex area of the brain, the better able you are to conduct higher-order executive functions such as goal planning and executing, self-discipline, and self-control. These attributes are needed to take advantage of the law of attraction because we must know what we want and what goal to set our focus on, sometimes to the exclusion of other goals.

The researchers identified a difference in reward processing in the structure and function of the brain in healthy individuals and the structure and function of the impaired brain of cocaine addicts. In the study, a monetary reward was on offer ranging from $0 to $50. The larger sums would be won by those who answered more questions correctly.

The researchers found that whilst the nonaddicts and addicts were in harmony in their statements regarding being motivated, excited, and interested in the task, this harmony did not correlate with the information picked up from their brains by the EEG.

The nonaddicts' brains displayed the expected increases in electrical signals emitting from the brain as they thought about winning more money, with the bigger the sums involved the greater the electrical activity. "The higher the grey matter volume in the reward centres, the more brain activity increased for the higher monetary rewards as compared to the no-reward condition."

In contrast, the addicts' brains did not replicate their stated intention. "The cocaine-addicted individuals had reduced grey matter volume in these regions compared with healthy subjects, and no detectable difference between the reward conditions in the… measurement of brain activity" (Parvaz MA, et al., 2012).

The electrical activity in an addict's brain was similar when aiming for $1 as it was when aiming for $50. Think about this: the order is important. To get excited about $50 takes more brain activity, so if they were as excited about $50 as they were about $1 this would be beneficial: they would be highly motivated throughout the whole task. However, being as excited about $1 as they were about $50, they were at low levels of motivation throughout the task. "These findings suggest that impaired reward processing may be attributed to deficits in the structural integrity of the brain, particularly in prefrontal cortical region implicated in higher order cognitive and emotional functioning" (ibid.).

The researchers draw from their findings that dysfunctional behaviours may be caused by structure-function deficits. These behaviours are demonstrated by a compromised ability to control behaviours and compulsions, make executive decisions, and follow through. The behaviours are exacerbated by stress.

What is important to us as we look for reasons we cannot manifest using a natural law is this:

The addicts said they were excited and motivated about earning $50. They said the higher the reward the more excited they became, the more motivated towards the goal and the more interested in succeeding.

That's what they *said*.

It is not what they *felt*.

They could not feel it enough to create the electrical impulses which would increase their brain activity and propel them to take action, engage more in the task, concentrate harder, answer questions faster, or maintain a high level of motivation. This is because they did not have the material in the brain to enable them to do so. They did not have as much grey matter mass, and therefore as many neurons firing as the healthy subjects.

In my own experience, repeatedly after I achieved a big goal I felt exhausted. Today I believe I do not have as much grey matter volume, and so I overstretched my capabilities. Somehow, I was able to temporarily push myself beyond my physical attributes. However, a consequence of this was that it resulted in a huge and unusual flood of chemicals and electrical activity to my wounded brain, probably causing further damage. I may have accessed this state because I tricked my brain into thinking it was in danger. Without being under specific pressure and with limited functioning of the brain, I could not on a consistent basis turn on the high stress levels, which were the only way I had learnt to motivate myself. My traumatised brain would only function in fight-or-flight mode. Calmness caused me anxiety. It triggered memories of my childhood home. Calmness was a prelude to something kicking off. Trauma, stress, and anxiety were familiar to me, and the only environment in which I could function. The only environment in which I truly felt safe.

Childhood abuse and trauma forces the body to remember, and live in, the way things were.

Chapter 8
The Suppression of Negative Emotions

For most of human history, the concepts of child abuse and childhood trauma didn't exist. Most natural philosophers believed that children were simply miniature, ignorant adults. If you were lucky enough to survive childhood without dying of an infectious disease, and you were not mentally ill, then you were just as good as anyone else.

A little over a century ago, Sigmund Freud first introduced the topic of childhood sexual abuse. In his paper *The Aetiology of Hysteria* (1896), Freud stated that the hysteria and neurosis of many of his patients (as he termed it) could be traced directly to the repressed memories of an early abuse. Based on what he was seeing, he was convinced there was an epidemic of child sexual abuse taking place within the homes in his country.

For his own reasons, Freud later modified what he called his seduction theory, which emphasised the causative impact of nurture: the shaping of the mind by experience. He then advanced the theory that his clients who spoke of abuse in their homes were merely expressing repressed fantasies rather than actual memories that were too painful to consciously tolerate.

The issue lay dormant until the publication of *The Battered Child Syndrome* by Dr C. Henry Kempe in 1962. Regarded as the seminal event in creating awareness and exposing the reality of child abuse, Kempe's paper gave doctors a way to understand and identify child abuse and neglect, along with information about how to report suspected abuse.

The ensuing outcry by adults who, as children, had experienced abuse by their parents led to the enactment of laws protecting the reporting of child abuse.

Today, episodes of serious neglect and physical abuse of children are featured regularly in the news. Sadly, researchers have found that dysfunctional childhoods are commonplace. Many adults need support while they address the suppressed memories that have resurfaced into their consciousness.

Whilst many leading thinkers in the field of the law of attraction field are aware of dysfunctional childhoods, there seems to be little awareness of how difficult it can be to overcome the lasting effects of ACEs. Here is a quote from Jack Canfield, in *The Secret* (2016):

"A lot of people feel like they're victims in life, and they'll often point to past events, perhaps growing up in an abusive or dysfunctional family. Most psychologists believe that about 85 per cent of families are dysfunctional, so all of a sudden you're not so unique. What do you choose now? Because you can either keep focusing on that, or you can focus on what you want. And when people start focusing on what they want, what they don't want falls away, and what they want expands, and the other part disappears."

It seems many promoters of the law of attraction are not aware of the deep effects of experiencing a less-than-optimal upbringing—but then neither were you, until now. Attracting what you want in your life is possible only if your own brain isn't fighting you. It's possible only if you don't have an invisible enemy trying to subvert your best efforts. It's possible only if your brain is properly wired to envision and embrace the good things you tell yourself you want.

A dysfunctional childhood can have an immense impact on the adult life.

"Our brains are sculpted by our early experiences," writes Martin Teicher (2000). "Maltreatment is a chisel that shapes a brain to contend with strife, but at the cost of deep, enduring wounds. Childhood abuse isn't something you 'get over.'"

This says it all.

In adulthood, the consequences of damage to the brain have been found to drive perfectionism, procrastination, anxieties, workaholism, and compulsive behaviours, whether shopping or substance abuse. It is difficult to think positive thoughts from a foundation of neglect.

Many of you reading this, I suspect, will not be willing to relate to it, believing that you did not suffer any kind of abuse in childhood, since you were adequately fed, clothed, and housed, and that your parents loved you. Some of you may be thinking that because you managed the house at age seven, and ensured your siblings went to school and did their homework, therefore you escaped unscathed.

This is rarely the case.

Perhaps, until reading this book, you will not have stopped to consider just how terrified and confused you were as a child. It is likely you will have suppressed these feelings for years and even decades.

Your Thinking Can Make You Sick

Some teachers of the law of attraction put childhood-based dysfunction and damaged thinking at the forefront. In her book *You Can Heal Your Life*, Louise Hay suggested that the underlying reason behind insanity and mental illness is the need to flee from the family, to escape and withdraw, and to violently separate from life. Furthermore, the reasoning behind the resulting addictive and compulsive behaviour is the suppressed need to run away from the self, fear, and not knowing how to love the self.

In contrast, *A Course in Miracles* (2008), called this fearful thinking a "miscreation." It states you "are passively condoning your mind's miscreations," and "Whenever you are afraid, it is a sure sign that you have allowed your mind to miscreate and have not allowed me [i.e., your God, your Higher Intelligence] to guide it."

From a metaphysical perspective, Louise Hay's book, *You Can Heal Your Life*, describes the negative perceptions behind illnesses:

Addictions
- Running from the self
- Fear
- Not knowing how to love self

Depression
- Anger you feel you do not have a right to have
- Hopelessness

Cancer
- Deep hurt
- Longstanding resentment
- Deep secret or grief eating away at the self
- Carrying hatreds

Lupus
- A giving up
- Better to die than stand up for one's self
- Anger and punishment

Liver
- Seat of anger and primitive emotions
- Chronic complaining
- Justifying fault-finding to deceive yourself
- Feeling bad

Insanity
- Fleeing from the family
- Escapism, withdrawal
- Violent separation from life

Some of her theories have been scientifically validated. The Blue Knot Foundation in Australia found research to confirm, "Childhood abuse increases the likelihood of growing into an adult who experiences depression, anxiety disorders, addictions or personality disorders" (Spila, et al., 2008).

The teachings of *A Course in Miracles* have also been verified. Gabor Maté states we are addicted to our stress hormones. We are so used to living in a state of high anxiety—our mind's miscreations—that we find peace stressful.

"For those habituated to high levels of internal stress since early childhood, it is the absence of stress that creates unease, evoking boredom and a sense of meaninglessness. To such persons stress feels desirable, while the absence of it feels like something to be avoided" (Maté, 2008).

This is exactly what Izidor said. Because of his childhood experiences, he felt more comfortable being attacked and unloved than in being loved. He became *angry* when he felt his adoptive parents loved him.

Negative Emotions Triggered

One may ask, to what place are negative emotions suppressed, and why is the mind miscreating? Take good note here that the emotions are not *dissipated* or *dismissed*. They are *suppressed*, which the Merriam-Webster Dictionary defines as, "the conscious intentional exclusion from consciousness of a thought or feeling."

If the thought or feeling is excluded from our consciousness, has it vanished? No, it has moved into our subconscious. If it's suppressed, it's a bit like a bulb planted in healthy soil that subsequently has a lump of concrete poured over it. The bulb tries and struggles, in vain, to grow. Eventually it gives up, and is forced to remain in the earth. With no healthy route to fulfil its normal life function, it becomes deformed, withers, and dies. If it were given a healthy route out, it would grow, flourish, and flower. It would reach its potential and in so doing, spread joy to others.

In *Why Love Matters* (2015), Sue Gerhardt suggests that negative emotions are "more suppressed than absent." She affirms the profound effects of early stress on a baby or toddler's developing nervous system. When a child has adverse experiences in early life, to survive he or she must adapt his or her behaviour, and the child's brain adapts too. Early stress particularly affects the brain's emotion and immune systems, and they can become less effective. As we saw in the story of Kurt Cobain, Izidor Ruckel, and countless others, this makes the child more vulnerable to a range of later difficulties including depression, antisocial behaviour, addictions, eating disorders, and physical illness.

Suppressing negative feelings doesn't make them disappear. This expresses the truth in a single phrase. Those unpleasant feelings, like the suppressed bulb, lie dormant. In a person, this state continues until a situation arises whereby another person, place, or thing triggers the dormant, unconscious ways of thinking and relating to others. We have seen over and over again that when people don't receive therapy for a traumatic event—such as the patients of Dr Felitti, who suffered in silence—then the negative energy erupts in some other way. Typically, it's either rage against others ("everyone's out to get me") or self-harm (abandoning oneself to addiction or other unhealthy behaviour).

This behaviour is based on defence. The fight-or-flight syndrome will result either in inappropriate behaviour such as sudden aggression or reverting mentally to a child, or the emotions will push to the surface. This creates discomfort, which the adult will try to regulate with substances or behaviours. Whether they choose drugs, alcohol, food, or any other self-abusive behaviour, while this self-medication calms them in the moment, they are ultimately emotionally disadvantaged. Their mental and spiritual state can range from unproductive to downright dangerous and destructive.

It Won't "Just Go Away"

Suppressing a feeling does not make it go away.

Many children unconsciously suppress their hurt and grief because their experience is too traumatising for them to confront in any other way. They rarely know any other way; they have little choice. They deal with their anxiety by seeking to minimise the threat and calm their emotional distress.

If you were a child growing up in a dysfunctional environment, you would probably want to flee the family, but you couldn't—after all, where could you go?

It is unlikely you could leave the family home. With a strong biological, food, and shelter dependency attachment to your parent or parents, you would not want to leave.

But as child, you do not understand these feelings intellectually. You are simply aware of a strong sense of love and loyalty. And if you cannot flee physically, then the next best place to flee is into your mind. You can escape and withdraw; you can separate yourself from life. This isn't a conscious decision. You do not deliberately seek to do this out of logical thought. It's a "passive miscreation," a strategy that becomes your mechanism for survival, and when you see that it works, it remains your mechanism for survival.

Physical, emotional or sexual violence are overwhelming experiences for children. They neither understand abuse nor do they have the physical resources to protect themselves. Trapped in a dangerous situation, children often respond to abuse with a "last ditch" psychological defence: they suppress their knowledge of the abuse. As the survivor grows, his or her knowledge of their abuse may remain "split off" from awareness, but it deeply shapes their thinking patterns and ways of relating to others.

Alice Miller in *The Truth Shall Set You Free* calls this "emotional blindness." It's an apt description. You can see from this how the default mechanism springs into action when you are an adult, directly developed from how you reacted as a child to a similar stimulus.

It is your complex trauma experiences together with the resulting suppressed memories that cause your mind to "miscreate" and attract lack and fear. You are either hypersensitive or shut down emotionally. This dictates your outlook on, and your ability to feel satisfied with, your life.

Pods of Stored Trouble

Think of memories as chemical and electrical "pods" of energy, stored around your nervous system like multiple chakras. However, instead of the familiar neat and tidy seven-chakra line-up, these pods of energy are randomly scattered like Christmas tree lights around your body—some flashing, some disconnected, some burnt-out, and all causing trouble.

Thus the memories surface in different ways, depending on what has caused them and what has triggered them. Hence, this is why some people get a stomach-ache when distressed, while others get head or neck pains or a sore throat. Metaphysically, it is demonstrated if someone did not get support as a child, they develop problems with their hips or their lower back. Many adults who have experienced childhood trauma have autoimmune issues such as thyroid dysfunction, lupus, and cancers. These are illnesses where the body is attacking itself. And, as Louise Hay and Bessel van der Kolk point out, they may be the body's physical manifestation of destructive beliefs and feelings of low self-worth.

It's not pleasant, is it? Not for those around you, and—more importantly—not for you.

If despite your best efforts your life is not what you wish it to be, you must look at the deeper cause for your lack of success using the law of attraction. This deeper cause is buried, like our analytical bulb, but longing to surface and flower, and suffering because it can't. And the truth is this: it is only you who is crushing it with your subconscious "stinkin' thinking."

Harsh, eh? It is what it is. No more dressing it up. The first step on the road to recovery is to face and accept reality.

It's All in the Brain

Freud spoke of "repressed" memories and fantasies. His tenet was that his patients were not fully aware of what was driving their thoughts and their mental distress. This was because the reasons were hidden in their unconscious, below their conscious awareness.

In the late 1800s, Émile Coué de la Châtaigneraie was the father of positive autosuggestion, and he highlighted the power of the subconscious in relation to positive and negative thinking. He wrote, "When the conscious (will) and subconscious (imagination) minds are in conflict, the subconscious mind will always—without exception—prevail." (1922)

When talking about repressed memories and mental illness, if we are going to really understand the power of the subconscious mind over the conscious mind, we need to look at the source: the brain.

Specifically, we need to look at how the brain suppresses the information we need to function optimally, or causes us to develop physical and mental illnesses. Then we need to look at how we can safely reverse this to allow us to find peace and purpose in our lives.

In his landmark 1937 work *Think and Grow Rich*, Napoleon Hill wrote, "Every brain is both a broadcasting station and a receiving station for the vibrations of thought. Whatever the actual science of thought transmissions may be, it is true that if you wish to receive the power contained in the thoughts of others, you must condition your mind to receive those ideas."

Again, he's saying that if your mind and heart are clogged with negative or painful thoughts from the past, or if your brain chemistry has been altered by ACEs or CPTSD, then it will not be capable of processing positive information that, if you are focused on success, you will embrace.

Hill's broadcasting station refers to the energetic links that exist both among humans and between humans and the universal source. It is this energetic link that makes us feel excited and positive among a cheering large audience—think football stadiums, or a seminar by an inspiring speaker. All our brains and nervous systems are concurrently firing off electrical and chemical signals to communicate with different areas of the body and with the universal source.

This connection can also precipitate mass hysteria. It is through the power of our brains to connect to each other, and to the source, that we attract and manifest as well as give support to others. This is the reason why it's difficult to replicate these heightened feelings when, afterwards, we are alone. The connection has been lost. It is a similar to the anomaly of going from a stadium floodlight to a candle.

There is another reason why the connections to universal source and to each other may be difficult to maintain. This is if the development of the structure of your brain has been disrupted due to the continual stress of growing up in a dysfunctional environment.

Jack P. Shonkoff and Andrew S. Garner (2012) write in "The Lifelong Effects of Early Childhood Adversity and Toxic Stress" that many adult diseases are in fact developmental disorders that have their roots early in life, and that "persistent health disparities associated with poverty, discrimination, or maltreatment could be reduced by the alleviation of toxic stress in childhood."

Given no other solution, it's inevitable that a child will manage his or her painful feelings and memories by suppressing them. If you cannot change your environment, and if you have no choice but to live with the parents or caregivers who provide you with the means to live, what other choice do you have? The unfortunate reality, however, is that those suppressed feelings of fear and anger will become the voice of the invisible enemy; and this enemy will tell you, year after year, that you are incapable of attracting goodness and positive energy into your life and it will control and direct your behaviour so it is congruent with such thoughts.

Chapter 9

Core Behaviours – Normal Reactions to Abnormal Situations

"An abnormal reaction to an abnormal situation is normal behavior."
– Viktor E. Frankl, *Man's Search for Meaning*

In an attempt to help you recognise or consider core behavioural symptoms that may be limiting your life, there follows detailed descriptions below.

Black and White Thinking

One core belief of the traumatised adult is that life is black or white. There are no subtle gradations of emotions or perceptions. There are no delicate tones of dawn or the silvery glow of the evening moon, only the harsh glare of high noon or the black shroud of midnight.

In more practical terms, your father is the guy who will beat you and then in the next breath tell you how lucky you are to be his son. Hot or cold—those are your choices. Nothing is ever pleasantly normal. You can never let down your guard, because pain can come at any moment.

This is a fear-based belief. It is when we jump to conclusions.

It's a primitive form of existence. Let's say that Stone Age man or Adam and Eve lived life with few choices:

Run from the sabre tooth tiger, or be eaten.

Do not eat the fruit from that tree, or eat it and be banished from Paradise.

As children, there are even fewer choices for us. We can hardly leave home and run from the "tiger." Or, if we tried to get the affection that is a child's birth right, our need for attachment was exploited, and we were abused, ignored, or chastised for wanting the fruit of the tree. We were effectively being punished for wanting love.

In my case I was a nuisance and always the source of someone's anger.

I was constantly told I was the reason why my mother had no money, so I grew up and created unmanageable debt.

I was constantly told I was too thin, my hair was too short, and when I developed anaemia… well… I had developed it to embarrass my mother. I grew up to have autoimmune illnesses.

Despite my best efforts, I was constantly told I wasn't good enough. In adult life, I confused my employees by being inconsistent with my standards of work. When I became more responsible, I ended up "shunned" by my employer—that is to say, my surrogate parent.

As adults, such beliefs can easily manifest into fight-or-flight and an unmanageable life. For me and many other people in the same situation, the result was self-perpetuating adult behaviour along similar lines.

In my case, I fled from one self-created disaster to another. I did not stop to consider that a situation could have many facets and therefore an abundance of options was available for dealing with it—far more and better options than fighting or fleeing. I had no staying power. I shunned the responsibility of making a life less ordinary for myself.

I was prevented from seeing the irrationality of my behaviour because my primitive brain assured me it was how a person needed to act to survive. This was because it had been grooved into my psychic a long time earlier: *in my childhood.*

Shame

One of the deepest scars for adults who suffer ACEs is that of having been made to feel shame for having needs. The needs were to have our feelings regulated and balance restored when necessary, and to be loved and cared for.

Diamond and Hopson (1998) say that in the first twenty-four months of life, personality, temperament, and emotional reactions are established. Since the area of the brain dealing with the emotional system develops faster than the prefrontal lobe that helps control those emotions, it is necessary that someone else's frontal lobe acts as a supportive scaffolding. As areas of the brain connect up, the child learns to control his behaviour. For example, as the child learns socialisation, he will do something the parent considers naughty. The parent will signal her disapproval. The child's brain releases stress hormones, which create a sense of what we have named "shame." This feels stressful, and the stress hormone cortisol is released in his brain. When the parent regulates the child swiftly and restores their connection, the stress hormone returns to a normal level. However, when a child is left in the state of stress too long or the child is embarrassed or ignored, the child becomes hypervigilant to avoid such shaming situations. He cannot develop emotional confidence. This can lead to the child growing into an adult who is "prone to depression—easily plunged into dysregulation by a current feeling of humiliation or loss" (Gerhardt, 2015).

Denial

A sad aspect of ACEs is the suppression of the memories that explain why we feel and behave the way we do. As a child, denial helped to keep you alive because it hurt too much to face the truth. It may be difficult for you to call your childhood experiences which led to trauma what they were—abuse, neglect, and abandonment. You may consider trauma only a fit description for children who had suffered in a war zone or who had had explicit sexual or physical abuse. However, your needs as a child are so finely tuned that any abuse, whether moderate or extreme, can unbalance the delicate developmental process. Denial can cause you to live as a "counterfeit adult." You are a high-achiever on the outside but frightened and distressed on the inside. Denial may not be recognised until you receive formal treatment.

Disassociation

Disassociation is a result of not having been wanted, protected, or loved. The consequences of not getting good enough care can lead to lifelong psychological distress. Your needs are dictated by evolution. The human baby continues to develop after birth, and brain and body development are dependent and influenced by the care received. So, what can happen when your evolutionary needs are not met?

If your need to have your feelings moderated appropriately are not met, if there is rejection or lack of interaction with the caregiver, your distress reactions split into two patterns of response.

First, you experience hyperarousal, and this is demonstrated in crying and screaming. Physically there is a rise in blood pressure and a drop in heart rate. As the period of nonregulation continues, you experience frantic distress. Your brain releases major stress hormones, signifying to you that you are having an unsafe experience.

As the challenging environment prevails, your response switches. You then disengage "from stimuli in the external world and attends to an internal world" (Schore, 2009). There is reduced emotional expression. You now feign death to conserve your energy. You "withdraw" from the helpless stressful environment. For a demonstration of this you can view Edward Tronick's still face experiment on Youtube.

Even though you have grown up and left the environment where the experiences took place, your brain is constantly processing them. The thoughts, feelings, and behaviours connected with your memories are stored in the brain in fragmented pieces. You can have a flashback to a memory or a feeling, or you can demonstrate a behaviour or experience physical pain but have no understanding of why or what triggered it. You just feel you are in danger.

Disassociation has been described as "staring off into space with a glazed look." This is also seen in adults who have experienced PTSD or childhood trauma. Behaviours learnt in childhood continue as a defence in adulthood. You now use this defence as you learned as a child: to help you "escape when there is no escape" (Putnam, 1997).

During this escape, the right brain loses its ability to act in an "integrated system." Integrated in the sense of being aware of the past, present, and future. You have "an immature and functionally limited right brain capacity to regulate… life stressors." That is, the parts of the brain that should work together to keep you connected with life are disrupted. There is a lot of impulsive behaviour, as the past is not used for guidance as to what not to do, nor are plans made in anticipation of the future. The consequence of not reflecting and not planning is that you are rendered "vulnerable to stress-related... disorders."

Co-dependency

The very nature of existence is relationships. In your childhood, your development and survival depends on having a strong secure attachment to another human. If this attachment need is not met, we take into adult life the urge at its basic form. This results in behaviours such as co-dependency—a way of living by linking our need for safety and wellbeing to the needs of our friends, our relationships, and even our work.

Charles Whitfield (2010) defines co-dependency as "any suffering and/or dysfunction that is associated with or results from focusing on the needs and behaviour of others." It is also defined as "an inability to maintain functional relationships." (CoDa 1999)

To get our needs met, we can abandon ourselves by tending to the needs of others and adapting to their needs while constantly seeking their approval and consciously living in fear of their disappointment, anger, or being abandoned by them. We have inability to say "no" to people and have little or no boundaries to protect us from other people's behaviour. Or we can manipulate others to give us what we want at that moment. This is rarely set out in an honest manner, i.e., "I am hurting and I would like you to help me." Rather we use arrogance or authority to control others. Hurting people hurt other people.

Obviously, any relationship with a hidden agenda (hidden even from the perpetrator) or an imbalance in power rarely functions effectively. Paradoxically we are on the right track, trying to interact with others and build relationships but in an unhealthy manner.

As one person seeking the right track said, "It seemed like when I was born, the doctor cut the umbilical cord, and I picked it up, endlessly trying to plug it back into someone or something to feel safe and connected again" (CoDa, 1999).

Fans of the law of attraction who come from dysfunctional homes find normal human relationships overwhelming. This is the result of damage in areas of the brain dealing with emotions and cognitive function: the ability to think things through and weigh up different options.

"After having been traumatized," wrote van der Kolk (2015), "the brain is re-set to respond to ordinary challenges as existential threats, and the body continues to pump out stress hormones that make people feel frazzled, agitated, or shut down. After the brain has been rewired to over-focus on danger it has trouble paying attention to subtle changes in one's universe."

Co-dependency causes us to continually demonstrate core behaviours to varying degrees. This is owing to the disconnection in our brain, which means we are living from a fear-based perspective. This leads to chronic unhappiness, compulsive behaviours, difficulty creating or maintaining functional relationships and even mental and physical illnesses (Whitfield, 2010).

Control

Rage, fear, and separation distress systems form at birth as emotional skills needed for survival (Sunderland, 2006). Responsiveness from a primary caregiver is essential to supporting the growing child as he learns how to calm himself until the prefrontal cortex is developed fully. The developed prefrontal cortex will give the child more complex emotional skills such as love, pleasure, happiness, shame, sadness, and guilt. A lack of responsive caring leads to a child, and subsequently an adult, with fewer response options when interacting with others. They resort to familiar survival tactics. They cannot apply the brakes to intense feelings or rage reactions because they have never been taught how to do so. The result is usually to display inappropriate behaviour.

To counter this, they may try to control other people to feel safe and avoid abandonment, or as a way to feel needed. As a child, we may have tried to appease a parent by being the "good girl" or "mummy's little helper." We may have taken on adult responsibilities such as supporting our siblings. This was a way to feel secure in an otherwise chaotic, inconsistent environment.

Controlling behaviour is a display of fear. It leads to stress and anxiety for those of us living with the consequences of a dysfunctional childhood. This behaviour rarely results in a positive outcome because we cannot control other people, we can only work on controlling ourselves. We get disappointed, anxious and angry, and lose our ability to be spontaneous.

Over-responsibility

Following on from our control issues, many of us take on adult responsibilities early in life. Usually, they were thrust upon us and we became the parent to our parents or our siblings. We became over-vigilant and continually on guard in case something terrible should happen to our family. We had all the answers and solutions. In adult life, we find we cannot say "no" to people's request for our resources. Though we may enjoy being busy and being needed, deep down we may fear being abandoned or disliked, so we stay responsible for others, ignoring our responsibility for ourselves. After relentlessly ignoring our own needs, we burn out or snap, and end up angry and hurt, the exact feelings we were trying to avoid.

Neglecting Your Needs

Over-responsibility is one way we neglect our needs. A child's basic needs are to have a secure framework from which to build confidence in regulating the ups and downs of life. If these needs are not met, the child and the resulting adult find it harder to cope effectively with stress, and will have little confidence in coping as an individual or trusting others as allies.

We are living with unfinished business. When our needs were not met as a child, we could not meet them ourselves. We could not regulate our own feelings. We became scared for our very survival and of these unresolved, unrecognised but deeply felt feelings.

"It isn't possible to generate the attitude of self-care and awareness of one's own feelings if someone else hasn't first done it for you," wrote Sue Gerhardt in 2015. "You need to have an experience with someone first… then you can reproduce it."

The lack of positive experiences in our childhood has caused us to live from a distorted stressed frame of reference.

As adults, we are seeking to be taken care of, "to have all wishes fulfilled by magic" (Gerhardt, 2015), and to have needs anticipated by others who should be mind readers. We can become "avoidant," making few demands to avoid being abandoned again, or maybe perfectionistic and uber-ambitious to find self-esteem. We are susceptible to addictions and illnesses, as the feelings which we have suppressed and forgotten swirl around us, clamouring for attention and resolution.

What we must accept is that we cannot use willpower to simply "change our thoughts, change our lives." Neither can we push away negative thoughts. To do so would need executive function skills such as detached observation and reflection. These skills are formed in the upper brain, in areas such as the prefrontal cortex. These are underdeveloped and damaged due to our ACEs. The damage also results in a lack of interaction between the brain areas, which required the experience of people responding to our needs and helping us learn how to regulate our feelings. We needed to have been supported when we were dependent so we could learn how to become independent (ibid.).

Fear

All the above core behaviour symptoms are demonstrations of fear. Fear permeates the life of an adult from a dysfunctional family living in a chaotic environment. Whether the chaos was subtle or overt, it was not conducive to a feeling of safety and security. The continual disappointments that came from a dysfunctional upbringing gave us the belief that bad things were always waiting to happen to us. Why? Because we were bad. We fear especially abandonment. So much so we will abandon others for no good reason in order to neutralise them before they hurt us. Fear is our unconscious defence mechanism and will be displayed as anger, rage or resentment, manipulation, deceit or anxiety, feeling uptight, or being highly sensitive. This way of life keeps us hypervigilant to protect ourselves from being shamed or hurt. This behaviour zaps our physical and mental energy: we are rarely in the present as to protect ourselves as we either focus on the past or project into the future.

Evolution leaves its mark too. When you feel threatened

by a colleague or other individual, you are likely to feel something on a psychological and biological level that's been hardwired into all of our brains since evolution: Fight-or-flight.

A dysfunctional family doesn't necessarily mean a family atmosphere filled with overt hate and daily aggression or addictions. When, as a child, you suffered a negative reaction from someone you trusted or turned to for love or support, even in a reasonably loving family where there was no obvious abuse, fear was triggered because the areas of the brain dealing with logic and rational thinking were not developed. If this occurred on a sustained basis, the fear became pathological. You were either always on the lookout for anyone trying to hurt you or you found yourself trying to please people to avoid any unpleasant situations. And as an adult, every time you meet a similar stimulus, it triggers the same response, however inappropriately.

We tend to exaggerate feelings or minimise them. We are hyperaroused or we suppress our arousal. We are either demanding too much of others or too little, simply because we have not mastered the process of self-regulation. In other words, we look for approval and love from outside.

With regard to manifesting using the law of attraction, the negative effect of this "all or none" thinking is that it limits our creativity, possibilities, and choices, and it restricts our ability to grow from experiences in our lives.

As you read my book and begin to heal, you will find that, simultaneously, you will begin to look at life and your experiences with shades of grey, instead of simply black or white.

Make the Invisible Enemy Visible

One of the saddest factors of childhood dysfunction and trauma is that you may not know until you start reading books like this that you experienced it. What happened at home was probably quite normal to you, especially if the dysfunction wasn't overt, such as sexual abuse. Even physical abuse can be interpreted as deserved, because you were likely to be aware of feeling shame about it, and because your caregiver told you that you deserved it. Yet underneath there will be a feeling of suppressed anger. This anger creates chemical and electrical impulses throughout the body, which make you tense, angry, resentful, and fearful. The anger then seeps out in inappropriate behaviour and reactions, which surprise and scare others... and you.

The Important Connection

Children need connections with others whom they trust. This is a primitive need. Generally, the people closest to them will be immediate and extended family.

In various ways, these people provide love, nurturing, and help to make a child feel safe and avoid harm. When these needs are not met, or there is a break or disconnection at some point in a child's life, this is the root point from which unhealthy behaviour may surface later in life. As an adult, we look for the same feelings of love and nurturing, although we don't consciously realise we are looking for the love we needed as a child.

This means that when an emotional stressor occurs later in life, it triggers the suppressed feelings connected to the original wounding experience which has not been addressed and dealt with properly, leaving us in a perpetual cycle of searching for what was lost. The bigger problem now is that we get stuck. We find we cannot move forward until our needs are met. Typically, as the body frantically tries to heal itself, we look for ways to meet these needs, such as excessive drinking, drugs, binge eating, sexual addiction, and other unproductive behaviours. The mind takes the body off-piste, desperate to resolve what has gone wrong and latching on to anything it's given, in hopes of relief.

When the body eventually implodes with ill health, relationship breakdowns, or mental illness, we head off in another direction, searching for a treatment or pills to heal what is going on at another level.

This is where the law of attraction is associated with childhood trauma.

The law of attraction is linked to overcoming something that happened when you were a young child, defenceless and needy. The experiences have struck you deaf, dumb, and blind. You do not see what is being shown to you, you do not hear what is being said to you, and you cannot voice your feelings. Everything is coloured and directed by your past experiences. In the confusion, at some point in growing up, your thinking became distorted. Now, as an adult, unable to feel good enough to achieve the abundance you crave in all areas of your life, the easy riches of the law of attraction seem feasible.

Millions of us yearn for the sort of cars, houses, and clothes that make up the lifestyle of the rich and famous. Ah, the bliss. With a photoshoot here, a tweet there, it looks effortless. A day's work in a simple click… Job done. Listen, not only are these guys masters of marketing, but they have a powerful belief that they deserve their riches and they do not want to work too hard for them. As Kourtney Kardashian said, "We all have different priorities, and working, it's not my top priority. It's never going to be."

That's the law of attraction in action. Don't be a hater. She has got it all. Isn't that what you want?

For you to think you can achieve this by positive thinking alone is a prime example of distorted thinking. Happiness doesn't come with a simple click, or because you keep seeing double numbers—16:16 or 1:1—or because your moon is aligned. It comes with some deep soul healing, some physical healing, some analytical thinking, and some work, before you will truly start to feel. Then you will change and then you will truly believe. It is then that the magic happens. The scales drop from your eyes, and as Napoleon Hill says in *Think and Grow Rich*, "A new world will unfold before you."

It begins with addressing your needs and supplying yourself with the love and attention that you did not receive in your childhood. It is through this work that you will find the reasons for the feelings of guilt, shame, and resentment that are blocking your access to the universal flow of abundance being enjoyed by so many throughout the world. Yes, you must do it. As unfair as it sounds, it really is up to you now. If not you, who?

Beyond Money

The law of attraction isn't only about manifesting financial abundance. It's about cultivating self-contentment at a deeper level. This may surprise you, because your most pressing issue may well be around money. Or it may be about overcoming depression, addiction, dependency, or some other erratic behaviour or physiological condition given a convenient label. And if you've got as far as middle age or older, you're even more likely to reject the notion that your childhood has anything to do with your current dilemma. After all, so far so good, and why would what happened decades ago have an effect, *now*?

Quite a lot, actually.

I want you to reap the benefits of having your feet firmly on the ground in some areas of your life, while you increase your faith in your belief that the universe can, and will, provide.

And the results are available to you.

Your Past Was Imperfect

A key concept you need to assimilate is that no matter who you are, your past was imperfect. The only difference between you and the person who isn't reading this book because they're too busy being successful is the *degree to which* your life was imperfect, and *in what way* it was imperfect.

Let's agree that your distorted thinking arose from receiving less than optimal care and support during childhood. To a child growing up in a dysfunctional environment, this is akin to an avalanche hurtling down a mountain heading directly towards them.

The dysfunctional environment leads directly to feeling fearful, suspicious of people, and mistrusting anyone who might offer to help. Or it can lead to the opposite: craving anyone's love and being too trusting. In a need to obtain comfort and to feel loved and needed, to avoid being abandoned, you allow yourself to be taken advantage of. You do this by trying to fix people or by unwittingly allowing others to abuse you while telling you either they love you, or they're doing it for your own good. You do not know when up is down and down is up.

What you may find hard to accept, and deeply disturbing,

is the fact that even moderate abuse and dysfunction on a sustained basis can damage the delicate structural development of a child's brain. And damage to the structure of the brain means damage to the functions of the brain.

The problem with damage to the brain function is that you cannot think properly, nor can you plan, visualise, hope, and dream.

And all this happens because of issues from your childhood that haven't been resolved; issues that are still sitting there as breaks in the link, causing a barrier to real, positive thinking and prosperity.

Your Thinking Has Made Your Life

Your life is not what you want it to be, and it is because you do not believe being successful and happy (whether financially or emotionally rich) is your destiny. You do not believe that someone like you can have a life filled with good things without going into bad debt, and instead you act, "as if." Up go the Facebook and Instagram images. Let's fool the world!

You aren't even fooling yourself.

If you felt unloved as a child, and you managed to cope with that feeling, then that will be your norm as you grow older. You will feel comfortable when you feel unloved. It's something you've been trained for. The invisible enemy will be satisfied.

Your beliefs drive your actions even if consciously they do not produce results that are in your best material interest. It is incumbent on you to identify these beliefs and act to neutralise them. When you have clarity about what you are thinking and why, you then have a blueprint to work with as you gently replace them with beliefs you *choose* to hold in your subconscious.

Chapter 10

How Your Brain Blocks Your Efforts to Use the Law of Attraction

In our Western world of abundance, it's surprising that so many of us think so negatively about our lives and the world in which we live. To justify this viewpoint, there would need to be something powerful blocking us from achieving our goals. This "blocker" must be hidden beyond our conscious awareness and control. Could this "something" be lying in an unconscious zone within us, stuck like glue, buried deep in our childhood?

Yes, it could.

Negative thoughts, beliefs, and behaviours prevent the law of attraction from working; and until this childhood trauma is addressed, you will not be able to consistently and systematically attract positive elements of action into your life.

Emotional pain is the residual memory of an ACE. It's lodged in your mind, causing you to live with your defences on high alert and feel constantly under threat. This causes you to misinterpret an expression, mannerism, or tone of voice. This way of living is so exhausting that your mind, desperate to help you, sends you off searching for relief to try and blot out the stress by using alcohol, drugs, or other addictions.

Lack of life skills in how to overcome your problems leaves you unable to properly express empathy, deal with problem solving, or possess the ability to abstract and conceptualise. No one taught you how to really live your life. Some people have been told they should have been born knowing, others were just ignored or were indoctrinated with cult or religious dogma, all of which are extremes, unproductive to the wounded adult.

Co-dependency. Mental Health America defines a co-dependent as someone with low self-esteem, who takes on the role of martyr and become enmeshed in other people's lives. This is because they feel rewarded and satisfied when they feel "needed" by others. Or they indulge in addictive or compulsive behaviours, looking outside themselves to feel good.

You must address childhood trauma issues, because the traits you've developed to survive your childhood home have distorted your thinking. And distorted thinking leads to delusional thinking. This, in turn, will limit the way positive intentions and experiences can gravitate towards you in a meaningful way. You think more in the realms of fantasy, with no foundation of fact or belief, nor any real sense of faith. As a child, you may have dreamed that someone would rescue you from your dysfunctional home. But no-one came. You lost faith and hope and resorted to your survival mechanisms. They got you through then, and surely they are all you need now—or so you believe.

Your soul knows you do not believe in your ability to manifest. It knows you are angry, lonely, and tired of trying, of living. It then attracts situations to comfort you, to keep your actions and thoughts congruent with your beliefs.

Overcoming the lingering effects of childhood trauma to

live the life you want is what causes the mental, emotional, and spiritual shift that makes manifesting using the law of attraction work. This book will show how exactly it is working for millions.

And how it will work for you.

Chapter 11
The Space Age of Abundance

In the last decade, the theory surrounding the law of attraction has exploded into the public's consciousness. To date, over thirty million people in fifty countries have bought *The Secret*.

The law of attraction states you are promised a rich store of whatever you want if you just focus your mind and visualise your desire. If these promises are to be believed, it should be as easy for you to reach your goals as it is for you to choose what you want to watch on Netflix.

Law of attraction teachings use the essence of visualisation techniques to convince the mind to believe what you want is already there. But there is an easier way to start to change your beliefs.

In August 2018, I sat in a car whilst the driver pressed a couple of buttons before letting go of the steering wheel and folding his arms. As we chatted about the weather, the car parked itself. It backed itself into an empty space, straightened up, and shut off its engine. Ten years ago, when *The Secret* was published, a car that could park on its own was the stuff of *Star Trek*, of woo-woo… of the law of attraction. Today, it's on a street near you. Little flying devices deliver our parcels, and the army has technology that can make a tank disguise itself to look like a Fiat Punto.

All this technological advancement has become so normalised that if you heard on the news that by next Christmas you'll be able to teleport yourself to Massachusetts, you probably wouldn't bat an eyelid. We have accepted, easily and effortlessly, that we are living in the space age, a time of stupendous manifestations of ideas into reality.

This technological development has led to a growth in jobs and capital, not only in the industrialised West but in China, India, and Africa. Billions of aspirational and hard-working people have entered the employment markets of IT, finance, and consultancy. In China alone, over the last twenty years there has been an 80 per cent increase in overall prosperity and abundance, exemplified by a corresponding increase in car ownership. In fact, both in terms of demand and supply, China is now the largest automobile market worldwide, surpassing the United States and the European Union. From a standpoint of law of attraction success, their wildest dreams are coming true.

Yet all these miracles are simply the manifestation of visions from humans like you. Why are some people creating the stuff of fiction while at the same time, over on Facebook, fans of the law of attraction are posting feelings of joy and pride because they manifested a free cup of coffee?

We live in an era of growing global wealth and technological advances that make amazing gadgets available to just about anyone. This is happening because enough people are able to visualise and manifest, through their work, the fruits of success. You deserve to share in this success. To accomplish this by using the law of attraction to focus your mind on your goal, you first need to "get your house in order" by identifying and treating the invisible enemy that's dedicated to keeping you safe but down.

Chapter 12
How the Invisible Enemy Holds You Back

Every human being deserves to love life and have a positive self-image. Your invisible enemy is trying to deprive you of the happiness you deserve—don't let it!

Take it one step at a time. There is a sea of riches out there waiting for you to scoop up and possess. When you make the first small step towards reaching out for them, you give yourself the mental and physical feeling of indulging yourself. You begin to get a taste of what the real experience will feel like. Then you take another step, and another, all the while keeping the vision of success in your mind. This will awaken the desire to increase your skills to go on and obtain it. Each step will make you more comfortable with the positive energy you're creating, and more determined to get more.

Experience Success

To access the experience of success, you need to be practical and resourceful. Instead of focusing on how to do something that's way out of reach, trivial, or useless, focus on a goal, or series of goals, that satisfy these three requirements:

1. It's useful. At this stage of your healing, do not aim for skiing in Aspen if you can't pay your rent. Do not play with your stupendous creativity; use it in a productive manner.

2. Make sure you're doing every day what needs to be done. Sure, you can write five pages every morning, spend ten minutes focussing on your vision board, and then have a bubble bath. However, these behaviours are not enough. They are to be done in addition to, not as a replacement for, your obligations in life. Keep your finances in order, eat good food, and ensure your clothes are clean, your shoes have no holes, and your home is tidy. As Jim Rohn said, "Everything matters." You are not special and different. It is vital you attend to doing first things first. You will find that ticking the mundane things off your life list builds your brain power and creates a psychic change in your attitude, which goes a great way to help you combat procrastination and anxiety and help you reach your goal and become the person you want to be.

3. Be sure to get help with reconciling and re-educating the invisible enemy seeking to derail your dreams. This book will give you information about group support.

The more you build your real-life goal muscles and add to your experience, the more you will find ideas starting to flow that can help you and help others.

You can't change other people or the physical world around you, but you can change what is going on inside you. To begin this process, start by identifying the invisible enemy lurking within you. Confront it and get the treatment you deserve. Learn to love yourself. Engage in pursuits that make you feel good. Tell yourself how well you are doing. Radiate positive energy out instead of closing in. Practice being present, observe yourself, and take satisfaction in your small successes. Then notice how your successes become bigger with a little more effort on your part. Celebrate as your life starts to evolve and blossom. As if you are a magnet, the right people and concepts will flow towards you because you already have the mental ability to recognise and embrace whatever it is that you want out of life. You are already a magnet.

Acceptance

In its *Big Book (2010)*, Alcoholics Anonymous has a paragraph on acceptance that's valuable for anyone struggling with an invisible enemy:

"And acceptance is the answer to all my problems today. When I am disturbed, it is because I find some person, place, thing, or situation—some fact of my life —unacceptable to me, and I can find no serenity until I accept that person, place, thing, or situation as being exactly the way it is supposed to be at this moment. Nothing, absolutely nothing, happens in God's world by mistake. Until I could accept my alcoholism, I could not stay sober; unless I accept life completely on life's terms, I cannot be happy. I need to concentrate not so much on what needs to be changed in the world as on what needs to be changed in me and in my attitudes."

And so, we start to work on changing you and your attitude. To do this you must learn who you are warts and all, accept who you are and decide who you want to be. Self-awareness is key to this endeavour.

Adult Child and the Child Within

The need for healing is imperative and a priority at this beginning stage of our work together. This is because as I stated earlier many fans of the law of attraction are admitting that they are suffering depression, anxiety, and compulsive behaviours. My theory states that many of these associates have had ACEs, the consequences of which make them unable to benefit from the law of attraction. To change this we must heal from within. I want to introduce you to the "adult child" and the "inner child."

The "adult child" comes out of the 12-step programme. Twelve-step programmes are based on Alcoholics Anonymous, and their programme of recovery for alcoholics. The form has been adopted to deal with other areas of compulsive behaviour. It transpired that families of alcoholics often behaved in similar fashion to the alcoholic himself. For instance, they too may be aggressive when challenged, or they may indulge in behaviours such as taking drugs, or they may recreate their childhood home by marrying an alcoholic. Growing up in an alcoholic home caused sustained stress to the children, which affected their ability to function when they became adults. Groups were formed to support family members of alcoholics. The members called themselves "adult children."

The "child within" or "inner child" is a phrase in therapy circles. The inner child is "ultimately alive, energetic, creative and fulfilled: it is our Real Self" (Whitfield, 2010). The inner child is our natural joyous state. However, when the inner child has not received nurturing "or allowed freedom of expression, a false self emerges." Consciously or unconsciously, the false self feels a sense of victimisation. People feel fearful, defensive, and sensitive to others, plus there is sensitivity to smells and sounds. The false self will appear positive and may even achieve worldly success. Yet, deep down there is a feeling of emptiness.

The false self engages in certain behaviours to keep up the barriers erected to protect the wounded child. However, these behaviours are inappropriate and counterproductive for the adult.

The Real Self is a healthy brainstem in communication with the emotional and logical areas of the brain. Remember, the brainstem is the only area of the brain fully formed at birth. It was formed by your Creator. This Creator deemed that there was a need for human contact and experiences for the other areas of the brain to be formed. Our ability to breathe, to sense fear, to cry for help and to cry for love, the essentials of life, were given fully formed to us by our God.

Joe Dispenza in *Evolve your Brain* (2007) states:

"Objective consciousness... the Zero Point Field. You and I are connected to that field, which affords us life through the midbrain, the cerebellum and the brainstem. This is the subconscious mind."

If we are connected to the field, to the universal source through a brainstem that is inflamed, hungry, scared, angry, and horny (Godin, 2010), how does this affect our goals as they come through? They come through battered, bruised, and burnt around the edges. No wonder we never feel fulfilled or that we've achieved anything; and then we find ourselves two weeks later looking for another way to stuff that gaping hole in our soul.

For this reason, you are cautioned against modalities such as lucid dreaming and mind-altering substances. You are cautioned also against long meditation retreats. Participants have recorded disturbing experiences they were not strong enough to navigate. This is no quick fix: slowly and safely at all times.

Dispenza further states, "The brain is... the physical

apparatus through which the mind is produced," and the "mind is the result of a brain that is coordinating thought impulses through its various regions and substructures." The brain has to heal so it can coordinate your thoughts and strengthen the links between the various regions and substructures; otherwise your fragmented mind will continue to feed you fragmented and distorted thoughts.

The brainstem is the mental, emotional, spiritual and physical manifestation of the inner child. It is the brainstem and the chemical and electrical reactions from it that cause that inner anguish, detrimental core behaviours, and the feeling of fear that comes up when your senior manager calls you in for a "catch up." The brainstem served its purpose when we were younger. It kept us safe, but as an adult it is causing us pain. It needs to be nurtured, acknowledged, and re-parented by the emotional and logical brain so we become whole, sane, and alive. With our brains working in unison, with our happy childlike, connected brainstem, we are no longer at loggerheads with everyone or hiding from everyone. We can now plan and execute goals. We can build up the motivation to follow through and we can build the relationships that make life worthwhile. We will become and attract what we are: people who are happy, healthy, joyous and free. We will become real.

Chapter 13
Time for Healing

"Where am I?" I said, squinting because of the harsh artificial light. I could make out my best friend sitting in front of me.

"You are in hospital," she said. "You collapsed."

"Oh," I said. Then oblivion.

The next time I awoke, a nurse was leaning over me. She asked me why I hadn't seen a doctor in fifteen years.

"Because I wasn't sick," I mumbled.

"You weren't sick once in fifteen years? Don't be ridiculous. Your red blood cell count is so low you're going to need two blood transfusions."

I was in hospital for two weeks and it took another two weeks to get back on my feet. The nurse was right. I was ridiculous. For the previous fifteen years, I had abandoned myself. Spending time in other people's lives and their business while my mind, body, and soul dwindled, stuttered, and failed from lack of care, nurturing, and nutrition. I didn't know better then, but as I lay in the hospital bed with just enough strength to stare at the bare white walls, I knew things had to change. Thus started my research and seeking, and my stumbling upon the knowledge I have shared with you.

I haven't been to the doctor in a long time, but if I did

feel unwell I would notice it and take action rather than push on through. In the meantime, my life follows the path I will now detail to you. I support others in a healthy, mature fashion—it's my passion. But first and foremost I support myself. Please consider the suggestions below for your health and your wellbeing.

Health Protocol

I list below details of alternative healing practices and some products of which I want to make you aware. You will see how these tie in with the principles in this book that advocate healing from a cellular level. Before embarking on any healing regimen, always seek the advice of your physician or other qualified health provider.

Richard Shultz www.herbdoc.com
Bowel Flush

A sluggish, constipated, swollen bowel, retaining pounds of old faecal matter, can either compress a nearby area causing disease, or emit infection and toxins which can affect and infect any area of the body.

No matter how far removed the problem seems from the colon, no matter how ridiculous it may seem to do a bowel cleaning program instead of brain surgery, cleanse the bowel first and see what happens. If you're like my patients, you will be thrilled with the results.

SuperFood

This food powder is a natural blend of algae, green grasses, vegetables and fruit. It is ideal for anyone wanting to include more vitamins, minerals, enzymes, and nourishing natural compounds into their diet every day or from time to time.

These foods contain high levels of vitamin B12 and vitamin B6 for normal energy and reducing tiredness and fatigue. Also for those who wish to support their immune system, psychological function (how they think and feel), and the health of the nervous system (great for people who are prone to worry or feel nervous). These nutrients also aid normal red blood cell formation, and with high levels of B6 in this product, may especially support women looking to optimise hormone regulation.

Udo Erasmus https://udoerasmus.com/
Fats That Heal – Udo's for Brain Function
The brain is around 60 per cent fat, so it really should come as no surprise that we need to feed it fats—essential fats, omega-3 particularly. Key reasons why essential fatty acids could help with brain function include:

Blood flow to the brain
Essential fatty acids improve the membrane function of every cell in our body. This includes the blood cells, which are then better able to carry vital oxygen to the brain for cognitive function and take away carbon dioxide waste.

Getting the message through efficiently
The soya lecithin works to strengthen the barrier around the nerve axons, known as the myelin sheath. The myelin sheath is essential to enable your nerve axons (the connecting links between the neurons) to conduct electrical charges within the brain and throughout the body's nervous system, and protects the charge from interference.

Stable energy release
Fat is an energy source that is stable, unlike carbohydrates that burn quickly and give an energy spike followed by a

crash. Fats burn slowly so last longer and maintain our energy levels for longer. They also keep us feeling fuller for longer—again, carbohydrates, once they quickly burn off, leave us feeling hungry and tired, and our concentration levels and mood often suffer.

Patrick Flanagan https://www.phisciences.com
Megahydrate
MegaHydrate is the key that unlocks the potential of water for nutrient replenishment and waste removal at the cellular level. In a state of dehydration, body cells cannot assimilate nutrients and remove waste. MegaHydrate:
- Lowers surface tension of water you drink, leading to improved detoxification
- Increases absorption of other supplements
- Reduces pain and inflammation
- Exhibits powerful anti-aging properties
- Removes heavy metals from the body
- Balances pH or alkalises the body
- Easily accesses all cells in the body

Michael Kiriac, PhD https://bionutrition.com
BioAlgae Concentrate F3
BioAlgae Concentrate is a complete, balanced and synergistic whole food composed of microalgae-based ingredients. BioAlgae Concentrate has a completeness, balance, and synergy not found in any single algae or other food supplements. Its thousands of nutrients occur in their natural form that your body can recognise. The result is a more powerful, rejuvenating, healing, and nourishing effect on the body and brain. The BSF Forte strength formula F3 is advanced nutritional support for health maintenance, prevention, anti-aging, immune system support, weight loss, dieting and fasting, for high performance in fitness,

bodybuilding and fast-track life, and for prevention of deficiencies and degenerative problems.

Three-part Treatment

I have put together a three-part process for you to use to get to know yourself.

This is a process to be conducted consistently over a twenty-one-day period. If you stop even at day twenty, you must start again.

The full treatment is:
- One hour of a twelve-step meeting three times per week
- Twenty minutes per day writing exercise
- Five to twenty minutes minimum per day in silent contemplation

That's it. I know it seems too simple. However, we do not want our fight-or-flight system to become triggered because of too many feelings coming up too quickly into our awareness. Neither do I want to swamp you with so many options you feel too overwhelmed and never get started. This is serious stuff. We are working on healing the very structure of our brain. To do this we have to re-parent ourselves, and give ourselves the essential nurturing and love we did not as a child receive. This is deep, deep work using compassion. It is imperative we do this work slowly but seriously.

1. Join a Twelve-step Programme

First, you are to join a twelve-step programme, such as:
- Alcoholics Anonymous; or

- Adult Children of Alcoholics and Dysfunctional Families; or
- Co-dependents Anonymous.

I have listed at the back of the book other programmes to attend if you are experiencing issues with money, substance abuse, relationships, sex, or experiencing stress due to other issues. Attend these meetings and the ones suggested above. Face-to-face is ideal. However, they do have telephone and online meetings available.

Join one of the suggested twelve-step anonymous programmes and attend six meetings. The meetings are run with strict boundaries of anonymity and privacy. Attend six meetings preferably within fourteen days but maximum within the twenty-one days. You can just sit and listen. When you sit down, say a silent prayer asking the universe to bring you a piece of wisdom during the hour, then relax. Feel any feelings that come up but do not leave the meeting. Feel the support of the group and give thanks: you are no longer alone. Remember to attend six meetings even if that voice in your head says not to.

Benefits of Group Therapy

"Self"-help is not for us. Doing it ourselves is what got us into our current mess in the first place. We need others. We need connection. In *Think and Grow Rich,* Napoleon Hill promoted the Master Mind as a vital step to riches. This is the real secret.

A psychoanalyst and student of Carl Jung named Trigant Burrow (1875–1950) coined the phrase "group therapy." His work focused on the equality of everyone in the group setting as opposed to the unequal position of therapist to client. "Every member of the group, including the analyst, is both an observer of his own processes and is observed by all the other members of the group."

In *The Brain's Way of Healing* (2015), Norman Doidge describes a study of guitarists playing music together. What the EEG picked up was that different regions of the brains of the musicians synchronised with the same regions in the other musicians' brains. He wrote, "the coordinated ensembles of the neurons within each player's brain were playing together with the ensembles of neurons in their fellow musicians/brains."

As we sit in a meeting, I believe the brains of all the attendees synchronise and become one whole "God" brain. It is then we hear something we never thought of before or we think of something that helps another attendee. Another major benefit to us is that the meeting provides a safe non-judgemental environment in which our true feelings will be heard for what may be the first time in our life by others and by ourselves.

2. Writing

Second, you are to spend twenty minutes per day answering the questions below.

Develop the practice of writing about feelings, people, situations and behaviour causing you concern. Try in your writing to keep the focus on what your own distorted thinking might be in connection with the trouble. Answer these questions once a day:
- What is causing you concern?
- What can you do about it?

3. Silent Contemplation

Third, you are to spend five minutes per day in silence with no phone, TV, or people. The aim is to become comfortable with our self and our thoughts. For some, this is a frightening prospect. We do not force thoughts or try to stop thoughts. It is a form of self-observation. It is also a time to let our brain know it is safe with us.

Five minutes is your starting point. You want to work up to twenty minutes or more each day. This is because it takes time for the brain to settle down. The Silva Method advocates an exercise of counting backward from 100, 50, or 25 to 1, as this quietens the mind in a steady controlled fashion. You can meditate and pray in that time if you want to on the issues that came up in your writing.

As I want to heal the primitive part of my brain, the part I was born with, in meditation I treat it as I would a little child. I say to thoughts that come up "hush," "it's alright," and "there, there," instead of "Ohm" or "Amen" or "Thank you." Further, as I am reconnecting with my inner child whom I abandoned for decades, I think it prudent to go gently. So instead of looking in the mirror saying "I love you" a million times a day, I looked into my eyes and said, "I care about you," and "I accept responsibility for you. Please let me know if there is anything I can do for you." Over time, I started to hear my inner child speak back to me, and I took notice. As she built up her trust in me we moved on to "I love you," but it took a few weeks before it felt natural and real from the inside.

Additional Work

To strengthen your prefrontal cortex, investigate analytic thinking books and tools. One is tool is the Law School Admission Test (LSAT). This is the zenith of logical thinking training. It may seem unattractive to you and it is very hard to grasp but do look into it. Practising LSAT exercises will give you a more rounded recovery.

Closing Thought

You are living in a traumatised and traumatising society. As I complete this book, the world is living with its own "invisible enemy" and fear is palpable in the street. The world is living as adult children have lived their life for decades: scared, distrustful, wanting someone to sort this all out for them and unsure of what the future holds.

What is clear there will be a future. What is clear is that crystals and vision boards will not be enough to navigate it. What is clear is the easy promises of current law of attraction teachings are now defunct.

This work is more pertinent that ever. You can live a life glorious and free. But you have to take the rough with the smooth, the dark with the light, and the positive with the negative. And to do this you have to heal yourself. You have to forgive yourself. You have to love yourself.

This will come with work, then with new beliefs, then with faith. You will have all you need and have the strength to work towards all that you want for you and for the world.

I leave you for now with the words of Jim Rohn:

"For your world to change, you have to change."

Appendix

CDC-Kaiser Permanente Adverse Childhood Experiences Study

Prior to your eighteenth birthday:

	Question	No	Yes
1.	Did a parent or other adult in the household often or very often... Swear at you, insult you, put you down, or humiliate you? or Act in a way that made you afraid that you might be physically hurt?		
2.	Did a parent or other adult in the household often or very often... Push, grab, slap, or throw something at you? or Ever hit you so hard that you had marks or were injured?		
3.	Did an adult or person at least 5 years older than you ever... Touch or fondle you or have you touch their body in a sexual way? or Attempt or actually have oral, anal, or vaginal intercourse with you?		
4.	Did you often or very often feel that ... No one in your family loved you or thought you were important or special? or Your family didn't look out for each other, feel close to each other, or support each other?		

5.	Did you often or very often feel that … You didn't have enough to eat, had to wear dirty clothes, and had no one to protect you? or Your parents were too drunk or high to take care of you or take you to the doctor if you needed it?		
6.	Were your parents ever separated or divorced?		
7.	Was your mother or stepmother: Often or very often pushed, grabbed, slapped, or had something thrown at her? or Sometimes, often, or very often kicked, bitten, hit with a fist, or hit with something hard? or Ever repeatedly hit over at least a few minutes or threatened with a gun or knife?		
8.	Did you live with anyone who was a problem drinker or alcoholic, or who used street drugs?		
9.	Was a household member depressed or mentally ill, or did a household member attempt suicide?		
10.	Did a household member go to prison?		
	ACE SCORE		

The CDC-Kaiser Permanente Adverse Childhood Experiences Study is one of the largest investigations of childhood abuse and neglect and later-life health and well-being.

For further information and analysis of different scores please visit https://www.cdc.gov/violenceprevention/acestudy/

Groups for Adult Child and Inner Child Issues
www.adultchildren.org
www.al-anon.org
www.al-anon.org/alateen – for teenagers
www.co-anon.org
www.codependents.org
www.workaholics-anonymous.org
www.r-a.org – Recoveries Anonymous

Money
www.debtorsanonymous.org
www.underearnersanonymous.org
www.gamblersanonymous.org

Sex
www.slaa.org
www.saauk.info
www.saa-recovery.org
www.recovery.org

Drugs
www.alcoholicsanonymous.org
www.drugaddictsanonymous.org
www.na.org

Food
www.foodaddiction.com
www.foodaddicts.org
www.oagb.org.uk

References

Agartz I., Andersson J., Skare S. (2001) Abnormal brain white matter in schizophrenia: a diffusion tensor imaging study. *NeuroReport* 12(10): 2251–2254

Ainsworth, M.D.S. (1973). The Development of infant-mother attachment, in Review of Child Development Research, eds Cardwell B., Ricciuti H. (Chicago IL: University of Chicago Press;) 1-94

Auerbach, R. (2014) Adolescent nonsuicidal self-injury: Examining the role of child abuse, comorbidity, and disinhibition. *Psychiatry Research* 220(0): 579–584.#

Ballard, C., Stanley, A. and Brockington, I. (1995) Post-traumatic stress disorder (PTSD) after childbirth. *British Journal of Psychiatry* 166: 525–528

Behrens, K. Y., Hesse, E., & Main, M. (2007). Mothers' attachment status as determined by the Adult Attachment Interview predicts their 6-year-olds' reunion responses: A study conducted in Japan. *Developmental Psychology, 43*(6), 1553–1567.

Berk, L. E., Mann, T. D., & Ogan, A. T. (2006). Make-believe play: Wellspring for the development of self-tegulation. In D. G. Singer, R. Golinkoff, & K. Hirsh-Pasek SOCIODRAMATIC PLAY 195 (Eds.), Play = learning: How play motivates and enhances children's cognitive and social-emotional growth (pp. 74-100). New York:

Oxford University Press. Bretherton, I., & Beeghly, M. (1989). Pretense: Acting "as if." In J. J. Lockman

Bunge, S and Souza, M. (2009) Executive function and higher-order cognition: neuroimaging. In LR Squire (Ed.) *Encyclopedia of Neuroscience*, Volume 1, Academic Press, pp. 111-116.

Chetty, S. et al. (2014) Stress and glucocorticoids promite oligodendrogenesis in the adult hippocampus. *Molecular Psychiatry* 19(12):1275-1283.

Children's emotional development is built into the architecture of their brains (2006) Working Paper 2 National Scientific Council on the Developing Child, Harvard University.

Coué, E. (1922) Self Mastery through Conscious Autosuggestion. Malkan Publishing Co., Inc.

Diamond, M. C., & Hopson, J. (1998). Magic trees of the mind: How to nurture your child's intelligence, creativity, and healthy emotions from birth through adolescence. New York: Plume.

Excessive Stress disrupts the architecture of the developing brain (2005) National Scientific Council on the Developing Child Working Paper 32, Harvard University.

Felitti, V. et al (1998) Relationship of childhood abuse and household dysfunction to many of the leading causes of death in adults the adverse childhood experiences (ACE) study. *American Journal of Preventive Medicine* 14(4): 245–258.

Fromkin V. et al. (1974) The development of language in genie: a case of language acquisition beyond the "critical period", *Brain and Language*, 1(1): 81–107.

Godin, Seth. (2010) Linchpin: Are you indispensable? How to drive your career and create a remarkable future. Penguin Publishing Group

Goleman, D., Boyatzis, R., & McKee, A. (2002). The new leaders: Transforming the art of leadership into the science of results. London: Time Warner Books

Grieve, S. (2013) Widespread reductions in gray matter volume in depression. *Neuroimage Clinical* 6(3): 332–339.

Gunnar, M. R. et al., (1996) Stress reactivity and attachment security. *Developmental Psychobiology Vol. 29, Issue 3. 191-203*

Heuvel, M. and Pol, H. (2010). Exploring the brain network: A review on resting-state fMRI functional connectivity. *European Neuropsychopharmacology : The journal of the European College of Neuropsychopharmacology* 20: 519-34.

Hillis S. et al. (2016) Global prevalence of past-year violence against children: a systematic review and minimum estimates. *Pediatrics*137(3), e20154079.

Kaufman, M. (2005) Meditation Gives Brain a Charge, Study Finds, Washington Post, Monday, January 3, p. A05

Kagen J, Herschkowitz N (2005) A young mind in a growing brain. Mahwah, NJ: Erlbaum.

LeDoux, J. (1996) The Emotional Brain. Simon & Schuster

Lutz, A. et al. (2004) Long-term meditators self-induce high-amplitude gamma synchrony during mental practice. *PNAS* 101(46): 16369–16373.

Main, M., & Cassidy, J. (1988). Categories of response to reunion with the parent at age 6: Predictable from infant attachment classifications and stable over a 1-month period. *Developmental Psychology, 24*(3), 415–426.

Netley C. (1972). Dichotic listening performance of hemispherectomized patients. *Neuropsychologia* 10: 233–240.

Nelson C. A. et al., (2014) Romania's Abandoned Children: Deprivation, Brain Development, and the Struggle for Recovery. Harvard University Press

Sunderland, M. (2006) The Science of Parenting. London: Dorling Kindersley.

Parvaz, M. (2012) Structural integrity of the prefrontal cortex modulates electrocortical sensitivity to reward. *Journal of Cognitive Neuroscience* 24(7): 1560–1570.

Putnam, F. W. (1997). Dissociation in children and adolescents: A developmental perspective. Guilford Press.

Schore, A. (2009) Attachment trauma and developing right brain: origins of pathological dissociation. In P. Dell & J. O'Neil (Eds), *Dissociation and the Dissociative disorders: DSM-V and beyond*, Routledge/Taylor & Francis Group, pp. 107–141.

Shonkoff, J. and Garner, A. (2012) The lifelong effects of early childhood adversity and toxic stress. *Pediatrics* 129(1): e232–e246.

Spila, et al., (2008) Abuse in childhood and mental disorders in Adult life. *Child Abuse Review* 17(2): 133-138

Teicher, M. (2000) Wounds that time won't heal: The neurobiology of child abuse. *The Dana Forum on Brain Science*, 2(4): 50-67.

Web References (Accessed 9 May 2020)

A Course in Miracles. https://www.miraclecenter.org/a-course-in-miracles/T-2.VI.php

As a Man Thinketh. http://www.gutenberg.org/ebooks/4507

Assaraf. J., Why The law of Attraction does not work for some people. https://youtu.be/KMtSMcLVl-4

https://www.livealifeyoulove.com/7-reasons-the-law-of-attraction-doesnt-work-and-how-to-get-it-to-work/

ACE study. https://www.cdc.gov/violenceprevention/acestudy/pdf/fhhflorna.pdf

ACEs High https://acestoohigh.com/2012/05/23/toxic-stress-from-childhood-trauma-causes-obesity-too/

Blavatsky, H.P. https://www.theosociety.org/pasadena/isis/iu1-10.htm

Cobain, Kurt. https://consumer.healthday.com/encyclopedia/depression-12/depression-news-176/even-in-his-youth-644949.html
https://web.archive.org/web/20040430011407/http://www.nirvanafreak.net/art/art8a.shtml

Kardashians. https://finance.yahoo.com/news/kourtney-kardashian-says-apos-keeping-100400495.html

Romanian Orphans

https://izidorruckel.com/meet-izidor/
https://www.npr.org/sections/health-shots/2014/02/20/280237833/orphans-lonely-beginnings-reveal-how-parents-shape-a-childs-brain

The lasting impact of neglect. https://www.apa.org/monitor/2014/06/neglect

https://www.washingtonpost.com/sf/style/2014/01/30/a-lost-boy-finds-his-calling/?utm_term=.133a74187459

Rohn. J., Everything matters https://youtu.be/pn-C7p3Fyog

The Quimby Manuscripts. http://newthoughtlibrary.com/quimbyPhineas/manuscripts/pages/quimby-manuscripts-194.htm

Tronick, E., Still Face Experiment https://www.youtube.com/watch?v=apzXGEbZht0
https://www.slideshare.net/AndriaCampbell/new-attachment-emotional-well-being-and-the-developing-brain-powerpoint

Suggested Reading

AA Big Book. (2001)

ACA Big Red Book. (2006)

Anonymous. *A Course in Miracles. (2008)*

Arrowsmith, B. (2012) *The Woman Who Changed Her Brain.* Simon & Schuster.

Azerrad, Michael. "Come As You Are: The Story of Nirvana." Broadway Books, 1993.

CoDa (1999) *Co-Dependents Anonymous.* Hazelden.

Dispenza, J. (2007) *Evolve Your Brain.* Health Communications, Inc.

Doidge, N. (2008) *The Brain That Changes Itself.* Penguin Books.

Doidge, N. (2015) *The Brain's Way of Healing.* Penguin Books.

Frankl, V. (2004) *Man's Search for Meaning.* Ebury Publishing.

Gerhardt, S. (2015) *Why Love Matters.* Routledge.

Hay, L. (2004) *You Can Heal Your Life.* Hay House, Inc.

LeDoux, J. (1996) *The Emotional Brain.* Simon & Schuster.

Maté, G. (2008) *In the Realm of Hungry Ghosts.* Vintage.

Mellody, P. (2003) *Facing Codependency.* HarperCollins.

Miller, A. (2001) *The Truth Shall Set You Free: Overcoming Emotional Blindness and Finding Your True Adult Self.* Basic Books.

Miller, A. (1998) *Thou Shalt Not Be Aware.* Pluto Press.

Miller, A. (2005) *The Body Never Lies.* W. W. Norton & Company.

Miller, A. (1990) *Banished Knowledge: Facing Childhoods Injuries.* Anchor Books.

Walker, P. (2013) *Complex PTSD: From Surviving to Thriving.* Azure Coyote.

Whitfield, C. (2010) *Healing the Child Within.* Health Communications, Inc.

Vaillant, G. (1998) *Adaptation to Life.* Harvard University Press.

Van der Kolk, B. (2015) *The Body Keeps the Score.* Penguin Books.

Lightning Source UK Ltd.
Milton Keynes UK
UKHW010759080121
376670UK00003B/847

9 781913 568122